"Life Is far too im
to be taken se.

Dear Traveller,

Travel and tourism are now the world's largest industry.

Thousands of books, magazines and television programmes offer bewildering varieties and standards of advice, and travellers face a seemingly endless choice of hotels. Hardly surprising, therefore, that many people end up with second best.

This guide aims to help those who prefer not to spend valuable time researching holiday and business destinations and simply want to travel now, today, with the assurance that the hotel they arrive at will be exceptional.

That's the reason why this guide is different.

It has sought out the very best, those rare places where excellent service, superb cuisine and beautiful surroundings have combined to create a unique experience, whether for the experienced traveller or the hard-pressed businessman.

It is a completely independent book, written objectively and fairly and with particular attention to detail. Examining more than 160 hotels in 53 countries, it recommends the best rooms and suites and the best restaurants nearby.
But it doesn't award points or stars; how can a city hotel be properly compared to one in the African bush? Each hotel is unique, but all are embassies of luxury, charm, courtesy and style.

We hope you enjoy them as much as we have.

Yours faithfully,

Stéphane Fruitier

Publisher

contents

europe

unitedstates

africa

caribbean

europe

schlossdurnstein

According to legend, Durnstein Castle was a source of inspiration for the Grimm brothers. This enchanting hotel, rising gallantly above one of the most romantic sections of the Danube, will make you a believer.

Built in 1630 in the Renaissance style and for two centuries the property of Princess Starhemberg, the castle was acquired by the Thiery family in 1937. Opened as a hotel in 1970, Durnstein today balances its elegant history with a family atmosphere and service suited to even the most fastidious guest.

While most of the forty rooms and apartments have been adapted to the personality of the building, they are furnished with pieces from various epochs and styles including Baroque, Empire and Biedermeier. Naturally, all are equipped with the latest in modern comfort and convenience.

The restaurant, with its stunning view of the Danube's Wachau gorge, has acquired a reputation for being one of the best in the area, thanks to superb cuisine and a wide selection of regional wines.

Golf enthusiasts will find many opportunities for play nearby. Add to this the outdoor/indoor swimming pool (certainly one of the most beautiful in Austria), sauna and Turkish bath... Durnstein Castle is truly a fairy-tale come to life.

facts
T 43 2711 212
F 43 2711 212 30
38 rooms and suites.
Singles/Doubles:
From ATS 1850 to 2300
Suites: From ATS 3800
Tax and service charge included.
Plan: CP
Open from April to November.
Airport: 100 Km

dining
The restaurant serves international cuisine.

recreation
Indoor and outdoor swimming pools and fitness centre.
18-hole golf course available nearby.

additional
24-hour room service.
Meeting and banquet facilities.
Concierge. Turkish baths.
Hair stylist.

facts
Kartner Ring, 16
T 43 1 501 100
F 43 1 501 104
96 rooms and 32 suites.
Singles/Doubles:
From ATS 4400 to 12 000
Suites: From ATS 14 000 to 39 000
Tax and service charge included.
Plan: EP
Airport: 30 minutes

dining
Imperial: gastronomic cuisine.
Bar Maria Theresia: for cocktails
and live piano music.

Imperial Café: for coffee and cakes
(the famous Imperial Torte).

recreation
18-hole golf course, tennis courts,
fitness centre and riding nearby.

additional
24-hour room service. Concierge.
Meeting and banqueting facilities.
Air-conditioning. Limousine service.
English butler service. News-stand.
Beauty salon. Hair stylist.
Opera and theatre tickets.

Vienna, an evening in 1873.

Franz Joseph: Well, my dear, what did you think of my inauguration party yesterday at the Imperial Hotel?

Sissi: It was simply wonderful, Franz! What a marvellous establishment! Mightn't we spend a little more time there to acquaint ourselves with all its wonders?

Franz Joseph: But of course! What a charming idea. Did you notice how exceptionally fine the furniture, the tapestries and the chandeliers were in the Blue Suite? What elegance! It was by far the most refined and reminded me of our own home. And when were you considering a brief visit? Why not this very evening?

Sissi: With pleasure! But first we are dining in our apartments.

Franz Joseph: But my dear, why delay a moment longer? The hotel restaurant is exquisite and the surroundings are absolutely charming. Let us go immediately! Make haste! I am longing to be there!

Sissi: Calm yourself, my dear. You have the impatience of a child. Sit a moment and have one of these delicious cakes while I prepare myself. I dare say the hotel will still be there in a century's time and just as excellent...

Opened just a few years ago, Anassa (Greek for 'queen') represents a new level of luxury rarely found on the beautiful island of Cyprus. Recreating a traditional village, the resort is situated to the west of Neo Chorion village near the Akamas peninsula, one of the most lovely and unspoilt parts of the island. In addition to spectacular springtime displays of wild orchids and cyclamen, Anassa prides itself on its wonderful and immaculate beach — a true rarity in this part of the world — and on a spa second to none.

The bedrooms are no less perfect. All are decorated in light colours and give onto private balconies with uninterrupted views of the Mediterranean. The remarkable luxury of the suites is underscored by the fact that most have private plunge pools.

The cuisine features local ingredients, seafood in particular. Add to this the fact that Anassa is family-owned (the Michaelides also own The Annabelle, the renowned five-star hotel in Paphos) and your expectations of quality and authenticity are sure to be surpassed.

In short, Anassa is a resort for all seasons, the ultimate retreat for lovers of luxury or anyone ready to let stress and worry be washed away by the best that man and nature have to offer.

facts
PO Box 66006
T 357 6 888 000
F 357 6 322 900
177 rooms and suites.
Singles/Doubles: From CY£ 115
Suites: From CY£ 345 to 1700
Plan: CP
Airport: 40 minutes

dining
Amphora: international cuisine.
Hélios: for Mediterranean contemporary cuisine.
Le Basiliko: for Mediterranean/Asian fusion.

Le Pelagos: Mediterranean cuisine. Three bars.

recreation
Three swimming pools (one indoor), tennis court, squash ,gymnasium, table tennis, sailing lessons and all water sports.
Two 18-hole golf courses nearby.

additional
Thalassotherapy Spa. Massages. Hydrotherapy. Children's activities. Babysitting. Boutique. Aromatherapy. Foreign currency exchange.

acts
33 Roland Gardens
44 171 370 6701
44 171 373 0442
52 rooms and suites.
Singles/Doubles: From GB£ 165 to 795
Plan: EP
Airport: 45 minutes

dining
Blakes Restaurant & Bar:
international cuisine.

recreation
Health centre, tennis courts
and jogging nearby.

additional
24-hour room service.
Meeting facilities.
Secretarial services.

Who would have thought that behind the facades of the Victorian houses of South Kensington would lurk a hotel of extraordinary extravagance?

In style, Blakes is the exact opposite of the minimalist Hempel Hotel (located, appropriately, on the opposite side of Hyde Park) but both have the same owner and designer, Anouska Hempel.

If the other five star hotels in central London are enormous, stately ocean liners, then Blakes is a luxury yacht.

The perfectionist Ms Hempel has created a treasure trove of self-confident and highly individual decors: blues, golds, ochres, purples and blacks are boldly matched. In the bedrooms, heavy silk curtains in warm and shimmering colours surround the beds but with so much to excite the eye, who wants to go to sleep?

Blakes feels as if the whole world has been plundered to add to its already eclectic and varied style. Here, there's a table from Rajasthan, there a rug from Iran or a desk from Russia.

In recent years, London has seen its share of new watering holes, yet Blakes' restaurant and bar remain highly popular. Outside, make it a point to book a table at either 'Club Gascon', 'The Real Greek' or 'Smith's of Smithfield'.

claridge's

A few hundred yards from Bond Street and Hyde Park, Claridge's is the choice of visiting dignitaries the world over. The fiirst indication that you have arrived at one of the most elegant addresses in London are strains of music wafting from the foyer where the hotel's resident orchestra plays.

The newly-restored rooms (in either Art Deco or Victorian style) are very large and equipped with latest in entertainment and communications technology. An exemple of the phenomenal service? There are bell-pushes to summon the chambermaid or other members of staff. Take one of the two penthouse suites on the top floor if you want to experience the best the country (and maybe the world) has to offer.

Every aspect of Claridge's is so marvellous that you could easily live here, is spite of the city's often dreadful weather. But a roaring fire and a reviving cup of tea are enough to make up for the rain and the damp.

Speaking of which, in the undisputed homeland of afternoon tea, Claridge's has raised serving it to the level of an art. In the reading room, staff in tailcoats and breeches will offer you a cup or a house cocktail.

facts
Brook Street
T 44 20 7629 8860
F 44 20 7499 2210
136 rooms and 56 suites.
Singles/Doubles:
From GB£ 315 to 345
Suites: From GB£ 515 to 2495
Tax: 17.5%. Service charge included.
Plan: EP
Airport: 40 minutes

dining
The Restaurant: one of the most fashionable places in London.
Claridge's Bar: Mayfair's newest meeting place.
Dinner-dances every Friday and Saturday evening.

recreation
New rooftop health centre.

additional
Meeting and conference facilities.
Concierge. Hair salon. Steam bath.
Theatre desk.

Facts

Christchurch Road
+ 44 1425 275 341
+ 44 1425 272 310
33 rooms and 19 suites.
Singles/Doubles:
From GB£ 395 to 530
Suites: From GB£ 630 to 845
Tax included.
Plan: EP
Airport: 30 km

dining

Marryat Room: celebrated for its international cuisine (closed lunch on Mondays).

recreation

Indoor and outdoor swimming pools and tennis courts, 9-hole golf course, fitness centre, croquet and billiards. Fishing, sailing, riding and shooting nearby.

additional

Conference and banqueting facilities. Room service. Spa. Sauna. Whirlpool. Massage. Steam baths.

Built at the beginning of the eighteenth century and facing a lawn seemingly made of velvet, Chewton Glen is a small, sublime manor in the English countryside amid seventy acres of meadows and gardens tended to perfection.

A few hundred yards from the cliff top, from which there are views across to the Isle of Wight, the hotel has a captivatingly relaxed and understated atmosphere. Here you will discover an extremely well-equipped spa, a very respectable nine-hole golf course, an outstanding indoor swimming pool with trompe l'œil frescoes designed by a renowned muralist and many other distractions.

But that's not all. Perhaps the chief attraction of the Chewton Glen is its restaurant. French chef Pierre Chevillard creates stunning and original dishes, a mix of the classical and the contemporary accompanied by wines (more than 400!) which are among the best from every country.

The bedrooms are impeccably decorated with fine paintings, exquisite antiques and an abundance of fresh flowers, all of which represent the epitome of English style. There are also balconies and terraces from which to enjoy stunning views of the park. The highly-professional staff are conscientious and attentive, so you will immediately feel at ease when you arrive.

Cliveden has far too much history and this guidebook too little space to recount all the glorious moments this stately home has witnessed since it was built in 1666.

But perhaps a succinct summary will give an idea. In the past the property has belonged to Frederick, Prince of Wales and to several dukes. Queen Victoria stayed here, as did Winston Churchill, Lawrence of Arabia, Charlie Chaplin and Rudyard Kipling, to mention just a few on a very long list of illustrious names.

You will inevitably be as charmed by the myths and stories from the house's past as you will be by its present, superb incarnation as a hotel, justly considered one of the best in Europe or even the world.

The place is extremely impressive just from the outside, but the inside?

Wood panelling, seventeenth-century tapestries, eighteenth-century furniture, period porcelains and silver, paintings by Constable and Sargent (depicting among others, Nancy Astor, a former owner of the building) — all this is simply part of what's in store for the guest.

Furthermore, from the moment you arrive, you will be bowled over by the service, French cuisine and sports facilities.

facts
Berkshire
T 44 1628 668 561
F 44 1628 661 837
23 rooms and 15 suites.
Singles/Doubles: From GB£ 385
Suites: From GB£ 445
Tax: 17.5%
Plan: EP
Airport: 20 minutes

dining
The Terrace: for English and international cuisine.
Waldo's: a more intimate dining room

recreation
Indoor and outdoor swimming pool, tennis courts, squash court, riding, fitness centre and gymnasium.
18-hole golf course nearby.

additional
State-of-the-art board rooms.
Spa. Children's activities. Helipad.

facts
Boulevard Kennedy
33 4 9361 3901
33 4 9367 7604
20 rooms and suites.
Singles/Doubles:
From FRF 2200 to 4150
Suites: From FRF 5500
Tax and service charge included.
Plan: EP
Open April to October.
Airport: 20 minutes

dining
Pavilion Eden Roc: French haute cuisine with a nice view over the sea.
Beach Bar: for light lunches.

recreation
Swimming pool, five tennis courts and water sports.

additional
Conference and banqueting rooms.
24-hour concierge.
Room service.
Dry-cleaning service.

Built in 1860 amid acres of coastal pines by Monsieur de Villemessant (then owner of *Le Figaro*, the French daily newspaper), the Hotel du Cap was originally a private holiday residence reserved for entertaining colleagues of the unconventional press baron.

Shortly after the inauguration of the villa, however, Villemessant changed his mind and thus was born a hotel which has delighted generations of travellers ever since.

The hotel's great style and elegance will satisfy even the most demanding of guests. As for the suites, between the sky and the sea, their luxury is dazzling, their comfort unequalled. Stay in one on the top floor of the Eden Roc wing to catch the view over the Lerins Islands.

Carved right out of the rocks, the swimming pool is sensational. Feet in the water, head in the clouds... in a word: bliss! Because of its isolation and privacy, many celebrities make the Hotel du Cap their temporary quarters during the Cannes film festival. Nevertheless, just a few years ago, Tom Cruise, Nicole Kidman, Sylvester Stallone, Clint Eastwood and Hugh Grant were trapped inside by a frenzy of paparazzi.

For nostalgics of medieval times (and other people as well!), the Château de Bagnols is a little paradise in the heart of the Beaujolais.

Good taste is evident throughout this thirteenth-century château, which has been modified over the years — a few changes during the Renaissance, many more in the eighteenth century.

Thanks to a wealthy English publisher, the château has undergone its largest renovation yet to become a very luxurious hotel After more than six million dollars of work, mobilisation of 400 local artisans and a wealth of patience (a crane was needed to install the marble bath in the apartment 'Aux Bouquets'), the hotel was ready for its first privileged guests.

All the bedrooms have been decorated with great care and are full of sumptuous velvets and shimmering silks, works of art and remarkable murals. The public rooms are not outdone: the great gothic chimney is one of the most beautiful ir Europe, the sofas date from the seventeenth century, the frescoes are originals and the swimming pool nestles among Roman ruins.

In short, this listed monument will undoubtedly stay in your memory long after other hotels have been forgotten.

facts
T 33 4 7471 4000
F 33 4 7471 4049
20 rooms and suites.
Singles/Doubles:
From FRF 2200 to 6500
Tax and service charge included.
Open April to December.
Plan: EP
Airport: 50 minutes

dining
La Salle des Gardes and Le Salon d'Ombrage: regional haute cuisine.
Le Cuvage: for light meals.

recreation
Outdoor swimming pool.
18-hole golf course and riding nearby.

additional
Conference room.
24-hour room service.
Boutiques.

hoteldupalais

hoteldupalais

facts
1, Avenue de l'impératrice
T 33 5 59 41 64 00
F 33 5 59 41 67 99
136 rooms and 22 suites.
Singles/Doubles:
From FRF 1260 to 2950
Suites: From FRF 2765 to 6350
Tax and service included.
Plan: EP
Closed in February.
Airport: 5 minutes

dining
La Villa Eugénie: for gastronomic fare.
La Rotonde : for lunch or dinner.

L'Hippocampe: for lunch around the pool.

recreation
Outdoor heated sea water swimming pool, fitness centre and pitching green. 18-hole golf course, tennis, surfing and horseback riding nearby.

additional
24-hour room service. Concierge. Meeting and banquet facilities. Air-conditioned rooms. Hair stylist. Boutiques. Sauna. Beaches. Casino nearby.

The hotel du Palais was built in 1855 as an imperial villa where Napoleon III and his Spanish wife, Eugénie, received friends. It became a hotel in 1893 and has been a favoured destination for generations of international travellers and sports enthusiasts alike. Overlooking the white sand beaches of Biarritz's coastline — where it is actually possible to surf — and the brilliant blue Bay of Biscay, this Belle Époque hotel is the epitome of opulence. The vision of it at twilight, illuminated against the deepening sky by hundreds of crystalline lights, is one you won't soon forget.

During the 1950s a famous decorator undertook a complete renovation of the Palais, maintaining its grand style and making it even today one of the most sumptuous residences in France. The breathtaking lobby with its grand staircase, sparkling chandeliers and marble columns hints at what awaits in the bedrooms; resplendent with second empire details, many include balconies facing the sea.

Of course, the extravagance extends to the dining room. In addition to superb French cuisine, 'La Rotonde' offers panoramic views of the ocean, framed by lavish draperies in ivory and gold.

An inside tip: the Hotel du Palais also serves a fabulous breakfast, best taken outside by the pool.

hoteldelacite

Mid-way between Bordeaux and Monte Carlo, Carcassonne is Europe's largest fortified citadel. Passing through its fortress walls onto the narrow cobblestone streets, one immediately feels transported back to the Middle Age.

Just beyond the ramparts, the Hotel de la Cité is a paradise for the lovers of medieval era. And yet with its solid stone walls dark wood panelling and stained glass windows, this unique hotel has the feel of a cosy country home.

Each of the elegant bedrooms and suites is individually furnished, but most have beamed ceilings, floral tapestries and carved four-poster beds with damask drapes. Try to reserve any of those from 202 through 216, as they command the best views of the city. In addition, a new villa consisting of a suite with a private terrace was recently opened.

The real *pièce de résistance* is the restaurant La Barbacane, whose Gothic rooms contain magnificent fireplaces — large enough to roast a pig in — high ceilings and cathedral chairs. The quality and presentation of the cuisine is nearly indescribable; suffice it to say that the kitchen is where many other master chefs have come to train.

Would-be lords and ladies will also delight in the spacious garden. Here you can relax with a drink while enjoying the view of the Basilica of Saint-Nazare, or take a dip in the heated pool (the only one in the citadel).

facts
Place de l'église
T 33 4 68 71 98 71
F 33 4 68 71 50 15
49 rooms and 12 suites.
Singles/Doubles: From FRF 1570
Suites: From FRF 2620
Plan: EP
Airport: 45 minutes

dining
La Barbacane: gastronomic cuisine.
Chez Saskia: informal bistro.
Le Jardin de l'Eveque:
al fresco dining.

recreation
Outdoor heated swimming pool.
18-hole golf course, horseback
riding and tennis courts nearby.

additional
24-hour room service.
Meeting and banquet facilities.
Concierge. Excursions.
Garage.

royalparcevian

facts
South shore Lake Geneva
T 33 4 50 26 85 00
F 33 4 50 75 38 40
130 rooms and 24 suites.
Singles/Doubles:
From FRF 1575 to 4330
Suites: From FRF 3870 to 14 600
Tax and service charge included.
Plan: MAP
Airport: 45 minutes

dining
Eight restaurants in the Domaine
provide meals to suit every taste.

recreation
Five indoor and outdoor swimming
pools, five tennis courts, 18-hole golf
course, squash court, fitness centre,
climbing, rafting, sailing and skiing.

additional
24-hour room service and concierge.
Meeting and banquet facilities.
Laundry and dry cleaning service.
Hair stylist. Casino. Turkish bath.
Massage. Steam rooms and sauna.
Baby sitting service on request.
Boutiques. Parking. Helipad.

It's difficult to say which is more impressive, the Hotel Royal or the park on which it is located — overlooking Lake Geneva — otherwise known as the Domaine du Royal Club Evian.
The spectacular hotel was built during the Belle Epoque for the pleasure of King Edward VII and has retained its majesty thanks to domed ceilings, colonnades and original frescoes found throughout. Each of the light-filled, gracefully decorated bedrooms offers a balcony and views over the lake or the surrounding mountains. In The Royal's Better Living Institute, you will find a refined and luxurious spa where Thai massage and shiatsu are amongst the numerous state-of-the-art health and beauty treatments offered. The Domaine, on the other hand, is a 42 acre park made up of perfectly manicured gardens, one of the most attractive 18-hole golf courses in Europe and even its own helipad. To say that it has something for everyone is an understatement; in addition to the exceptional range of available sports there is a casino and a special children's club offering an impressive range of activities.
Guests have complimentary access to the Domaine and all its sporting opportunities, making the Hotel Royal the perfect choice for a comprehensive and unforgettable holiday.

lachevred'or

Without question, the Chateau de la Chevre d'Or's most memorable asset is its heart-stopping panoramic view over the Cote d'Azur.

Clinging to a hillside in the medieval village of Eze, this remarkable hotel stands high above the Mediterranean Sea. Whether you are in the dining room, at the terrace pools or in the bedrooms, the vistas are truly incredible.

Eleventh-century stone houses were converted to make up the hotel, so the bedrooms are scattered among different buildings. Individually styled, all of them are extremely comfortable and convey the rustic romance of days gone by.

The restaurant, run by Jean-Marc Delacourt, offers Mediterranean-inspired cuisine and a wine cellar stocked with rare vintages and a wide selection of cognacs. There is also a sister restaurant in the village itself (plan to walk there; because its ancient streets are so narrow, Eze is closed to cars.)

To lounge next to one of the Chateau's two swimming pools (even the 'lower' one is at 1,300 feet!), taking in the bougainvillea, the pungent scent of wild rosemary — and did we mention the view? — is to experience the French *joie de vivre* in its purest form.

facts
Moyenne Corniche
T 33 4 92 10 66 66
F 33 4 93 41 06 72
22 rooms and 9 suites.
Singles/Doubles:
From FRF 1700 to 3800
Suites: From FRF 3500 to 16 000
Plan: CP
Closed from end of November to 15th of March.
Airport: 20 minutes

dining
La Chevre d'Or: for French haute cui
L'Oliveto: for Italian and Mediterranean cuisine.
Le Grill du Chateau: for salads and g

recreation
Outdoor heated swimming pool.
18-hole golf course, tennis, sailing and water sports nearby.

additional
Room service. Concierge.
Meeting and banquet facilities.
Air-conditioning. Parking.

facts
Route de l'Abbaye de Senanque
T 33 4 90 72 00 51
F 33 4 90 72 01 22
27 rooms and 2 suites.
Singles/Doubles: From FRF 960
Suites: From FRF 2580
Service charge not included.
Plan: EP
Airport: 30 minutes

dining
The cuisine is Provencal
and international.
Bar.

recreation
Outdoor and indoor swimming
pools and tennis courts.
18-hole golf course nearby.

additional
Room service. Air-conditioning.
Meeting and banquet facilities.
Boutiques. Parking. Garage.
Health institute. Massage.

The picturesque village of Gordes is quite popular at the moment, due to Peter Mayle's books about Provence. Perhaps not as well known, but well worth discovering is a charming hotel there called Les Bories.

Named after ancient, beehive-shaped shepherds' dwellings found in the area, the building and its grounds are like a mirage in a region otherwise known for its stone buildings and rocky terrain. It is one of the few places in France you can float in a spectacular swimming pool and gaze up at a massive mountain — in this case Mount Ventoux, whose white crest makes it look snow-capped even in summer.

Air-conditioned and spacious bedrooms feature fresh, contemporary decor. Their floor-to-ceiling windows open onto private terraces — the perfect place to put your brain on pause and experience the important things in life: the sound of crickets, the feel of sunshine, the gentle scent of wildflowers in bloom.

When the most important thing becomes dinner, the cosy, fire-lit dining room — designed to create the experience of being inside a borie itself — offers the finest of regional specialties and an extensive selection of local wines.

To borrow a word from Mr. Mayle, you will find you could easily spend a year here.

aubergedecassagne

On the outskirts of the medieval city of Avignon, the Auberge de Cassagne occupies a grand chateau dating back to 1850.

This plus its proximity to some of the world's most respected vineyards is reason enough for a visit, but the Auberge's unbeatable combination of top-quality service and bucolic charm is what places it above all other hotels in the area. Once over the threshold, guests are plunged into a warm and harmonious atmosphere. A gate in a high wall leads to the garden, where plane trees shade the restaurant terrace and paths wind through greenery and flowers to the pool. The relaxed feeling continues into the bedrooms, all of which feature regional antiques and intimate porches with pool or garden views. Their fresh Provencal prints remind you that you are in the heart of a region famous for some of the most beautiful fabrics since the eighteenth century.

Last but certainly not least, the Auberge owes its culinary reputation to head chef Philippe Boucher, who has presided over the kitchen since 1983. Gourmets — hotel guests and locals alike — keep coming back for a taste of his traditional yet innovative cuisine which makes the most of the wonderful local produce.

facts
T 33 4 90 31 04 18
F 33 4 90 32 25 09
35 rooms and 5 suites.
Singles/Doubles: From FRF 850
Suites: From FRF 1880
Service charge not included.
Plan: EP
Airport: 30 minutes

dining
The cuisine is Provencal
and international.
Bar.

recreation
Outdoor swimming pool
and tennis courts.
18-hole golf course nearby.

additional
Room service.

facts
2–8, rue du Bœuf
T 33 4 72 77 44 44
F 33 4 72 40 93 61
63 rooms.
Singles/Doubles:
From FRF 1200 to 3000
Plan: EP
Airport: 40 minutes.

dining
Five dining rooms Including a new
restaurant, Les Loges, serving
creations of a young Breton chef,
Nicolas Le Bec.

recreation
Heated indoor swimming pool.

additional
24-hour room service.
Concierge. Boutiques. Hairdresser.
Conference and meeting facilities.
Jacuzzi. Sauna.

La Cour des Loges occupies four of the oldest buildings in Lyon's oldest quarter. Ranging from the fifteenth to seventeenth centuries, they originally belonged to the Duke of Burgundy, were next converted into a Jesuit college and then private apartments before an extremely creative renovation team turned them into one of the newest and most unique hotels in France. Three levels of Florentine arcades, ancient stone walls and an enclosed spiral stair contribute to an historical setting where it's easy to imagine Renaissance figures once wandering the corridors. Inside, modern elements and contemporary art blend perfectly with massive wooden beams and stucco walls rubbed with the deepest, most wonderful colours you can imagine.

Sixty-three rooms, suites and apartments combine similar modern decor with high-tech comfort. Double windows block city noise, automatic shutters control the light, and bathrooms feature enormous illuminated bathtubs.

'Les Loges', the most formal restaurant, is a masterpiece, both for the innovative cuisine of its Breton chef and its sensual design. Lyon being France's capital of gastronomy, you'll have no trouble finding places to eat outside either. Aim high for one of the city's landmark restaurants (concierge Gérard Ravet may be able to help with this) or try one of the *bouchons*, age-old taverns that promise good food, copious wine and a chance to dine with the locals.

What has always most compelling about Megève is its air of authenticity; it is this that continues to draws tourists and ski buffs to its snow-covered slopes.

Hoteliers and natives Jocelyne and Jean Louis Sibuet knew that a resort of such calibre would not stand for a hotel that did not match its true character. Thus they created an exquisite establishment that embodies the great tradition of Savoy hospitality.

In the heart of town, Les Fermes de Marie (named after the Sibuet's daughter) breathes warmth and good taste. Within its walls, furniture made smooth as silk by the patina of time, four poster beds and rich fabrics create a welcoming atmosphere, accentuated by subtle lighting.

'La Ferme de Beauté', the hotel's spa, boasts the latest technological innovations and personalised care under the guidance of professionals to help you find peak form.

In short, for a stay in the mountains where the refinement matchs the comfort in every area, look no further.

facts
Chemin de Riante Colline
T 33 4 50 93 03 10
F 33 4 50 93 09 84
69 rooms and suites.
Singles/Doubles:
From FRF 1200 to 2100
Suites: From FRF 2640 to 3540
Tax and service charge included.
Plan: CP
Airport: 60 minutes

dining
The chef expertly prepares dishes based on regional produce.
Bar.

recreation
Swimming pool, fitness centre, ski and winter sports.

additional
Room service. Spa. Concierge. Meeting facilities. Massage. Sauna. Dry-cleaning. Garage. Parking.

facts
Route de Bonnieux
T 33 4 90 72 30 20
F 33 4 90 72 54 20
8 rooms and 4 suites.
Singles/Doubles: From FRF 2000
Suites: From FRF 3500
Tax and service charge included.
Plan: CP
Airport: 100 Km

dining
The restaurant offers the freshest
local cuisine.

recreation
Two swimming pools.
18-hole golf course and tennis
courts nearby.

additional
Room service. Boutiques.
Excursions on request.

La Bastide de Marie, ideally located between Gordes and Bonnieux in the heart of Luberon National Park, is one of the most splendid properties in southern France. Surrounded by nearly forty acres of vineyards, this eighteenth-century house is a standing invitation to discover the subtle pleasures of Provence.

In the eight rooms and four suites, colours sing like cicadas. Sunflower yellow, aster mauve, wild anise green — each adds to the ambience and inspiration that seem to intensify with every moment of the day.

Opportunities to unwind are endless. You could pause for an aperitif in the shade of the big lime tree, discover local gastronomy exalted by herbs from the 'savoury garden' or walk among the vines that gave birth to the 'Domaine de Marie Marie' sampled the previous evening.

You might also follow the lead of many guests and venture out to browse the region's many antique shops, or simply take advantage of the hotel's two swimming pools to cool off after a day basking in the sun.

La Bastide de Marie doesn't bother to advertise, as it relies on word of mouth. So tell your friends — or don't, if like many who have discovered this pastoral hideaway, you'd prefer to keep the secret to yourself!

Named after its creator, the very famous hotel de Crillon was born at the same time as the magnificent Place de la Concorde.

Built during the reign of Louis XV in 1758, the hotel has preserved the splendour of the era. It is very fashionable, very classy and very formal. Heads of state (Helmut Kohl and Vaclav Havel, among others), celebrities (Harrison Ford and Michael Jackson), ambassadors and dignitaries — the Crillon has looked after them all.

The exquisite rooms mix silks and furniture of the rarest quality with fantastic decor. Overlooking the monument and offering an unbroken view over Paris towards Les Invalides, rooms 547, 549, 553 and 555 and their terraces are captivating. Rooms 101 and 158 are equally recommended; they have a different style with eighteenth-century panelling.

And what about the traffic noise in Place de la Concorde? Simply not a problem. All the rooms are equipped with the most modern windows, designed to prevent even the smallest noise from disturbing you.

With ultra-professional, discreet and charming staff and service, the whole experience cannot be faulted.

facts
10, Place de la Concorde
T 33 1 4471 1500
F 33 1 4471 1502
120 rooms and 43 suites.
Singles/Doubles:
From FRF 2600 to 4200
Tax and service charge included.
Plan: EP
Airport: 35 minutes

dining
Les Ambassadeurs: haute cuisine.
L'Obélisque: for French cuisine.
The Piano Bar: for perfect business appointments or cocktails.
The Jardin d'Hiver: for tea.

additional
18th-century meeting and conference rooms. Concierge. 24-hour room service. Boutiques. Business and secretarial services. Fully air-conditioned.Parking.

hotelritz

acts
5, Place Vendôme
33 1 4316 3030
33 1 4316 3668
35 rooms and 40 suites.
Singles/Doubles:
from FRF 3000 to 5000
Tax and service charge included.
Plan: EP
Airport: 35 minutes

dining
Espadon: French haute cuisine.
Bar Vendome: in summer, tea and
cocktails are served in the garden.

The Ritz-Club and Bar Hemingway:
for cocktails.

recreation
Indoor swimming pool, squash
court and fitness centre.

additional
24-hour room service.
Conference and banqueting facilities.
Business centre. Secretarial service.
Beauty salon. Babysitting.
Sauna. Massage.

Opened in 1898 by Cesar Ritz himself, the legendary Ritz inhabits one of the most chic districts of the French capital, only a few minutes' walk from the famous Opera Garnier and the Louvre museum.

In this incomparable eighteenth-century palace, rich curtains and draperies, sparkling chandeliers and an atmosphere of unashamed opulence are surpassed only by the Louis XV and XVI-style furniture in the rooms and public areas.

Each of the one-of-a-kind suites is testimony to the magnificence of France's hotel tradition; the 'Chanel', so named because Coco made the Ritz her personal residence for over forty years, is a true work of art. So, for that matter, is the Imperial Suite.

Part of the Ritz Health Club and surrounded by frescoes and mosaics, the indoor swimming pool resembles Roman baths and is certainly one of the most beautiful in the world.

It goes without saying that service here is outstanding, but some members of the staff are positively clairvoyant. Bar waiters have been known to commit one's drink to memory after just one visit!

Should you choose to dine outside the hotel, 'Pierre Gagnaire' and 'Guy Savoy' are among the best restaurants in the City of Light.

levallondevalrugues

Saint-Rémy-de-Provence is one of the most famous villages in a region that has inspired painters and other artistic souls for centuries. It is home to a delightful hotel that is sure to inspire you, too.

The Hostellerie du Vallon de Valrugues occupies a splendid villa of Roman origin. Its architecture is the only Italian thing about it though, for this hotel is a monument to the French *art de vivre*.

Its proximity to Aix, Nîmes and Arles (site of the Van Gogh Art Centre) means a wide choice of cultural excursions.

You might also spend a lazy afternoon on the lawn learning pétanque, the game of bowls that was once France's national pastime (pre-football, that is).

Simply decorated, rooms and suites offer the utmost in creature comforts. Many have terraces affording views of the nearby Alpilles and Luberon range. The most deluxe have private jacuzzis, and the Prestige Suite, its own swimming pool. Here you will faced with just one dilemma, and that is: where to partake of the fabulous Provencal cuisine? In the magnificent dining room or under the mulberry trees next to the pool? However you decide, the creations of Laurent Chouviat — an artist in his own right — will awaken your palate with the freshest flavours of the area.

facts
Chemin Canto Cigalo
T 33 4 90 92 04 40
F 33 4 90 92 44 01
38 rooms and 15 suites.
Singles/Doubles: From FRF 880
Suites: From FRF 2680
Service charge not included.
Plan: EP
Airport: 15 Km

dining
The cuisine is Provencal
and international.
Bar.

recreation
Outdoor swimming pool,
tennis courts, fitness centre,
golf practice and putting green.
18-hole golf course nearby.

additional
24-hour room service. Boutiques.
Meeting and banquet facilities.
Sauna. Massage. Jacuzzi.

chateaud'esclimont

facts
T 33 2 37 31 15 15
F 33 2 37 31 57 91
53 rooms and suites.
Singles/Doubles:
From FRF 1000 to 5200
Tax and service charge included.
Plan: EP
Airport: 45 km

dining
The restaurant serves the finest
French cuisine.

recreation
Outdoor swimming pool, pitch and
putt, horse riding and tennis courts.
18-hole golf course nearby.

additional
Room service. Parking. Helipad.
Meeting and banquet facilities.

Built for the Archbishop of Tours in 1543, the Château d'Esclimont is an excellent choice for anyone who wants to sleep and dine like royalty. Hidden off a small country road 40 miles south of Paris, its private drive winds through handsome gates to expose a stunning castle framed by trees and reflected in a beautiful lake dotted with swans.

Set in the middle of a 150-acre estate with French-style gardens, the Chateau is a vision of towers, balconies, turrets and pinnacles. A former residence of the La Rochefoulcauld family (whose motto, "*C'est mon plaisir*" — It's my pleasure — is still inscribed above the entrance) it has over the years also been home to many aristocrats, statesmen and politicians. The interiors are a fine example of Renaissance elegance where old and new co-exist quite comfortably.

You can choose a room in the Chateau itself or the Tower or the Hunting Lodge, but all of them are lavishly decorated with beautiful coordinating fabrics and reproduction eighteenth-century furniture.

Furthermore, the cuisine is outstanding. Served in the magnificent dining room (where you can gaze upon the swans) and accompanied by an impressive 400-vintage wine list, it is guaranteed to transport you to new heights of pleasure.

hotelbyblos

Saint Tropez, the provincial village that became famous in the '50s thanks to Brigitte Bardot, among others, sees its population increase a hundredfold every summer. Needless to say, finding a bit of peace and quiet here is quite a challenge. Happily it's one that the Hotel Byblos meets brilliantly.

Recalling a Mediterranean village, the hotel's architecture reflects the charm of the area and lets guest feel quickly at ease. Praise for this must also go to the wonderful service and relaxing rooms with their balcony views over the swimming pool and flower-filled gardens.

The surrounding area's most beautiful beaches (Club 55, Voile Rouge) are nearby, and in the evening the famous night-club 'Les Caves du Roy', which stays open until dawn, is within walking distance.

St. Tropez remains one of the best places on earth to watch the 'Beautiful People' at play... and everyone else, too! So if you intend to stay for a while, don't make the mistake of hiring a car. The traffic is so appalling you'd be better off on two wheels. Do not leave the village without visiting the wealthy museum 'l'Annonciade' and tasting the *bouillabaisse* 'Chez Camille' at Ramatuelle.

facts
Avenue Paul Signac
T 33 4 9456 6800
F 33 4 9456 6801
52 rooms and 43 suites.
Singles/Doubles:
From FRF 1300 to 4150
Suites: From FRF 3600 to 9700
Tax and service charge included.
Plan: EP
Open April to mid-October.
Airport: 60 minutes

dining
Le Byblos: gourmet restaurant
by the swimming pool.
Le Relais des Caves du Roy:
French-Italian brasserie.

recreation
Swimming pool and fitness centre.
18-hole golf course and water sport
nearby.

additional
Meeting rooms. 24-hour room service.
Boutiques. Sauna. Massage. Piano Bar
Turkish bath. Hairdresser. Beauty salon.

facts
T 33 3 80 62 89 98
F 33 3 80 62 82 34
39 rooms and 9 suites.
Singles/Doubles: From FRF 640
Suites: From FRF 1480
Tax included.
Plan: EP
Airport: 20 Km

dining
Le Clos Prieur: for French specialities.

recreation
Outdoor heated swimming pool, tennis court, table tennis and petanque.
18-hole golf course, horse-riding, squash and fishing nearby.

additional
Meeting and banquet facilities. Helipad. Excursions. Parking.

Like the vintage wines of Burgundy, the Chateau de Gilly gets better and better with the passage of time.
The main building, a rough-cut stone castle, was originally built for the priors of the Cistercian abbey in the fourteenth century. During the seventeenth century it was transformed into a lavish residence, and finally into a hotel in 1988.
Surrounded by vineyards, facing geometric gardens 'a la Française' and encircled by a moat, this hotel's history and architecture perfectly reflect the spirit of its region. Bedrooms and suites are welcoming and luxurious, appointed with such details as chandeliers and, depending on the room, fireplaces.
Going from one of the Chateau's buildings to another will give you the feeling of having stepped back in time. For instance, the restaurant is housed in a fourteenth-century former storeroom connected to the main building by tunnel. There, below vaulted stone ceilings and by the glow of candle and firelight, you will relish the outstanding cuisine of chef Christophe Barnouin accompanied by a generous variety of locally-produced wines.
Activities around the hotel? Many, including golf and cultural tours. Of course, one of the best is to wander the local vineyards with someone you love...

kroneassmannshausen

Near the Lorelei, where according to legend sailors were lured to their deaths by sirens, the Krone Assmannshausen stands on the banks of the Rhine as if painted there.

With its spiral turrets and wooden balconies, this hotel's exterior gives the impression of a Germanic castle of days gone by. Inside it is more like a grand family home, filled with comfortable furniture, pastoral paintings and photographs — which makes perfect sense, considering it has been run by the same family for four generations.

Though the oldest part of the building dates back four hundred and fifty years, there is nothing old-fashioned about the Krone Assmannshausen of today. The hotel was redecorated not long ago, at vast expense and with great panache.

The result is unbelievably sumptuous rooms boasting antiques and rich fabrics, each one different from its neighbour. Fresh flowers, French doors, four-poster beds and opulent marble bathrooms add to their enormous character.

But the real heart and soul of this hotel is the restaurant. Thanks to many outstanding vineyards in the area, its wine list is second to none. And the cuisine —authentic, substantial and light at the same time — is simply *wundervoll*.

facts
Rheinuferstrasse 10
T 49 67 22 40 30
F 49 67 22 30 49
65 rooms and suites
Singles/Doubles: DEM 185 to 350
Suites: from DEM 390 to 850
Plan : EP
Tax and service charge included.
Airport: 40 minutes

dining
Two restaurants serve classic cuisine with regional and Mediterranean influences.

recreation
Outdoor swimming pool.
18-hole golf course and riding nearby.

additional
Room service. Meeting facilities.

facts

Schillerstrasse 4-6
T 49 7221 9000
F 49 7221 3877 2
68 rooms and 32 suites.
Singles/Doubles:
From DEM 330 to 980
Suites: From DEM 1100 to 5100
Tax and service charge included.
Plan: EP
Airport: 90 minutes

dining

The Park restaurant: for
international cuisine.
Intimate bar for dancing.

recreation

Indoor swimming pool and fitness
centre.
18-hole golf course, tennis courts,
riding, fishing, hunting and hiking
nearby.

additional

Party and conference rooms.
Full Spa with exclusive suite.
Sauna. Steam-bath. Solarium.
Casino nearby.

'The best hotel in the world' according to Frank Sinatra, who knew a thing or two about enjoying himself. It is tempting to believe, for its architecture and surroundings lend Brenner's Park an exceptional atmosphere.

The hotel feels like an ocean liner in the middle of a park, such is its level of grandeur and refinement. Fabulous public rooms, sumptuous bedrooms and apartments in shades of orange with superb sheets and dressing tables — all blend to give the whole a dignified and elegant feel.

Dining is varied to suit all tastes and styles: there are light and quick meals and of course, feasts when you are feeling more indulgent. If you do find yourself over-doing it in the restaurant, remember that the city is famous as a health resort and has received for more than a century visitors from all over the world eager to try its waters.

This is one reason why the hotel frequently organises, in co-operation with body-care experts Villa Stéphanie, 'beauty weeks' — specialist programmes with a personal trainer to help you get in shape.

A standard-bearer for all hotels, Brenner's Park is perhaps the best in Europe.

hotelbrandenburgerhof

A few steps from Berlin's Kurfürstendamm and the Memorial Church, the Hotel Brandenburger Hof will delight lovers of both classic architecture and modern design. This turn-of-the-century Wilhelmian mansion opened as a hotel in 1991. Under the direction of proprietess Daniela Sauter, its total renovation resulted in a captivating mix of seemingly divergent styles.

Guests enter through an elegant neo-classic lobby leading to the Wintergarten, an open-air space resembling both an Italian monastery courtyard and a Japanese garden. Filled with plants and natural light, it is an ideal spot for a light meal or cocktails. Just beyond that is 'Die Quadriga', where you can indulge in Michelin-starred cuisine while sitting on Frank Lloyd Wright chairs.

In contrast to the timeless feel of the public areas, rooms are designed in ultra-sleek Bauhaus style. Lamps and furniture by Mies van der Rohe and Le Corbusier among others — many of which are on permanent display in New York's Museum of Modern Art — contribute to the refined and restful atmosphere.

From reception to the restaurants to the comprehensive spa, the staff is warm, discreet, and ready to spoil you rotten. All of which helps to explain why, in less than a decade, the Brandenburger Hof has become one of the most exclusive addresses in Germany's most cosmopolitan city.

facts
Eislebener Strasse, 14
T 49 30 214 050
F 49 30 214 051 00
78 rooms and 4 suites.
Singles/Doubles: From DEM 280 to 465
Suites: From DEM 745
Tax and service charge included.
Plan: CP
Airport: 20 minutes

dining
Die Quadriga offers classical grande cuisine in elegant settings (1 star in the Michelin guide).

Der Wintergarten : for regional French cuisine and afternoon tea.
Piano Bar: for cocktails with live piano music.

recreation
18-hole golf course, fitness centre and tennis courts nearby.

additional
Fully-equipped meeting and banquet facilities. Concierge. Parking. Beauty and massage institute Thaleia with steam bath and solarium.

schlosshugenpoet

dining
The renowned restaurant offers
superb gourmet dining.

recreation
Tennis court.
18-hole golf course nearby.

additional
24-hour room service. Concierge.
Conference and meeting facilities.

Dating back to 1647 and complete with a moat and a working drawbidge, Schloss Hugenpoet offers a glorious opportunity to experience life in an authentic Renaissance castle. This extraordinary hotel, surrounded by deep forests in the picturesque Ruhr River Valley, welcomed its first privileged guests in 1955.

Some of the interior features are older than the structure itself, having been salvaged from another, earlier castle. The magnificent black marble staircase and sandstone fireplaces alone are from the 1570s and considered amongst the most splendid ancient decorative works in the Rhineland.

Many other precious items, including tapestries, paintings and valuable antiques, can be found in the twenty-five guest rooms. Beautifully coloured and recalling the ambience of earlier centuries, they are also equipped with all modern conveniences.

The classically elegant dining room specialises in superb French-inspired cuisine, complimented by a cellar with over three hundred vintages, including some of the finest German white wines.

An excellent staff and familial atmosphere will make you feel immediately welcome. Who would expect less from such a distinguished establishment whose name translates into 'toad pool'? (Ask when you get there.)

kivotosclubhotel

Standing as an oasis of tranquillity on magnificent Ornos Bay is the Kivotos Clubhotel, a luxurious resort that perfectly embodies the special architecture of Mykonos.

Its brilliant white exterior is impressive enough, but the unique details found inside are what will most impress you. Everywhere you look — and a couple of places you wouldn't think to — are antiques and contemporary works of art produced by famous artists and craftsmen.

Forty-five sea-view rooms and suites are outfitted with the latest hotel equipment and every deluxe amenity. Tile floors, arched doorways and beamed ceilings contribute to their authentic, elegant feel.

In addition to two swimming pools (one sea-fed), a fitness centre and squash court, water sports are available at the nearby private beach. For something really special, a motorised yacht can be chartered for trips to neighbouring islands.

When it comes time to play tourist, the towns of Hora (known for its colourful harbour, cubist houses, winding streets and numerous tavernas) and Ano Mera (quieter, more traditional and site of a historic monastery) are a few just kilometres away.

facts
Ornos Bay
T 30 289 24094
F 30 289 22844
40 rooms and suites.
Singles/Doubles: From GRD 58 000
Suites: From GRD 134 000 to 258 000
Tax included.
Plan: CP
Airport: 4 km

dining
La Meduse, Mare and Le Private restaurants boast outstanding gastronomic tastes from all over the island.

recreation
Two swimming pools, water sports facilities, fitness and health club and squash court.
Riding, fishing, watersports and scuba diving nearby.

additional
Room service. Air-conditioned rooms. Meeting and banquet facilities.
Sauna. Jacuzzi. Massage room.
Boutique. Excursions.
Satellite Television.

facts
Nikiti 63088
T 30 375 223 10
F 30 375 225 91
58 rooms and suites.
Singles/Doubles: From GRD 48 000
Suites: From GRD 68 000 to 220 000
Service and taxes included.
Plan: EP
Airport: 95 Km

dining
The Squirrel: Open air, cliffside restaurant for fine dining.
The Grill: Beach side restaurant for lunch and Macedonian dishes.

The Pavillon: for breakfast.
The Sea Bar and The Pool Bar: for all-day cocktails and drinks.

recreation
Outdoor swimming pool, tennis court, boating, diving, fishing and fitness centre.

additional
Room service. Air-conditioned rooms.
Meeting and banquet facilities.
Sauna. Jacuzzi. Massage.
Boutique. Laundry and pressing.
Transportation desk. Valet service.
Butler service on request.

Considered one of the finest getaways in Greece, the Danai Beach Resort offers secluded luxury and attentive service in a spectacular natural setting. Perched on a bluff on the scenic Sithonia Peninsula, the resort comprises seven elegant villas set amidst acres of lush gardens where playful squirrels and songbirds are regular visitors. Each houses a number of spacious rooms and suites featuring neo-classic decor and a variety of deluxe amenities. All have music systems, most have jacuzzis, and several have large terraces facing the Aegean Sea.

For some particularly stunning visuals, choose one of the four suites with its own private swimming pool. In them, the only thing separating you from your pool and the azure water beyond is a glass wall with a fireplace in the middle.

Golden sand and a natural fringe of pine trees make the private beach a perfect spot for discreet sunbathing (a variety of watersports are also available).

From romantic, cliffside Mediterranean dinners to sumptuous breakfasts, the Danai's three restaurants offer something for every taste and mood. Not to mention that at almost any time you can sit with a cocktail or aromatic Greek coffee on one of the many peaceful verandahs and count yourself among the happy few…

katikies

You know the picture. Chalk-white cliff dwellings, shot from above, offset by a vast expanse of impossibly blue sea. You may not know you're looking at the Greek island of Santorini, but you think: 'Someday, I've got to go there'.

When that day comes, there is only one place you should stay.

Perched on the rim of a volcanic crater 300 feet above the sea, the Hotel Katikies is a fantasy of stairways, bridges and cave cottages with vertigo-inducing views — the result of an inspired mix of modern and traditional Aegean design.

The guest quarters rely on simple, rustic furnishings and plenty of light and fresh air to create a restful, romantic atmosphere. Equipped with modern facilities, all have a terrace or balcony.

The most spectacular is number 25 with its sensational views, a four poster bed and a stunning bathroom with hydromassage jet and a jacuzzi. The spectacular infinity pool is another vision sure to linger in your memory. Balanced on the edge of the caldera itself, it gives the illusion of merging into the sea. Understandably, most of the public activity takes place outside, where candlelit gourmet dinners are served in the open-air restaurant and sunset wine tastings initiate guests to the island's best vintages.

After a stay at Katikies you'll go home with a refreshed spirit and a new mantra: 'Someday, I've got to go back'.

facts
Oia
T 30 286 71401
F 30 286 71129
22 rooms and suites.
Singles/Doubles: From GRD 55 000
Suites: From GRD 75 000
Tax included
Plan: CP
Airport: 20 minutes

dining
Kirini: for Greek and international fare.
katikies restaurant: for wonderful
Mediterranean gourmet Cuisine.
Pool bar.

recreation
Two swimming pools.
Fishing and boating nearby.

additional
24-hour room service. Travel desk.
All accommodations with air
conditioning. Air-conditioned shuttle.
In-house laundry and pressing.
In room safe. Open-air Jacuzzi.
Massage and treatments.
Library with internet facility.
Excursions.

marlfieldhouse

facts

County Wexford
T 353 55 211 24
F 353 55 215 72
14 rooms and 6 suites.
Singles/Doubles: From IE£170
Suites: From IE£ 295
Tax included.
Plan: CP
Closed from mid-December to February.
Airport: 80 Km

dining

The restaurant offers superb modern Irish cuisine.

recreation

Tennis court and croquet on the grounds.
Horseback riding and many 18-hole golf courses nearby.

additional

Meeting and conference facilities.
Sauna. Parking.

Only ninety minutes south of Dublin stands Marlfield House, a Regency-style mansion preserving all that is cherished in the great tradition of Irish country houses.

Built in 1820, the hotel was part of the Courtown Estate and later became the principal Irish residence of the Earls of Courtown. In 1977 it was acquired by the Bowe family, who not only restored and redecorated the existing building, but added six luxurious state rooms and a magnificent conservatory dining room.

In addition to antiques that Mary Bowe has been collecting for the past thirty years, paintings, tapestries and fine Irish linen accentuate the bedrooms. Each has its own marble fireplace and is decorated in a different period style. Choosing one is a dilemma, but all are extraordinary; huge and airy with soaring ceilings, yet warm and so comfortable they become home in the blink of an eye. Some have views over the lake and wildfowl reserve.

The stylish curvilinear conservatory dining room is the perfect venue in which to enjoy the hotel's excellent cuisine. Featuring herbs and vegetables from Marlfield's own garden, it highlights local delicacies such as oysters and wild salmon. The hotel is also a perfect location from which to explore beauty spots such as Wicklow, Wexford and Waterford. Do go.

fourseasonsdublin

The first Four Seasons to open in Ireland is set among the ivy-covered residences of Ballsbridge, the most upscale quarter of Dublin. Occupying a three-and-a-half acre landmark site on the grounds of the Royal Dublin Society, the hotel is just minutes from the city centre with its shopping and historical districts. Wherever you'd like to go, the especially-resourceful concierge will be happy to point you in the right direction.

Over two hundred luxurious rooms in a variety of categories feature Georgian and Victorian décor, the chain's trademark huge bathrooms and tranquil views of the ornate courtyard or tree-lined streets of the neighbourhood. All of them are extra-spacious, and the Premium and Presidential Suites large enough for entertaining.

The elegant Seasons dining room offers contemporary European cuisine based on seasonal Irish produce and is a good choice for a special lunch or dinner. The Café offers a relaxed alternative and the chance to sample updated Irish favourites. The hotel also features a full-service fitness facility with indoor lap pool and jacuzzi.

Anyone visiting Dublin will be delighted with the Four Seasons, but pint-sized travellers may get a special kick out of it. Not only are children welcomed with an amenity, but bedtime milk and cookies, child-sized bathrobes and video game units are available.

facts
Simmonscourt Road, Ballsbridge
T 353 1 665 4000
F 353 1 665 4099
259 rooms and 67 suites.
Singles/Doubles: From IE£ 280 to 375
Suites: From 475 to 1495
Plan: EP
Tax and service charge icluded.
Airport: 45 minutes

dining
Seasons restaurant serves regional and international specialties.
Tea and beverages in the Lobby.

recreation
Swimming pool and fitness centre.
Horseback riding, tennis courts and 18-hole golf course nearby.

additional
Meeting and banquet rooms.
Extensive Health Club. Spa. Massag
Sauna. Aromatherapy. Beauty
treatments. No-smoking rooms.
24-hour concierge and room service
Hair salon.

facts
Ormond Quay
+ 353 1 887 2400
+ 353 1 878 3185
91 rooms and suites.
Singles/Doubles: From IE£ 175 to 350
Tax and service charge included.
Plan: EP
Airport: 14 km

dining
Halo restaurant serves modern
Europe cuisine.
The Morrison Bar & Café Bar.
Lobo: for late night supper bar and
restaurant.

recreation
Sports can be easily arranged.

additional
Air-conditioned rooms.
CD players.

Dublin's South Side has been 'happening' for some time now, but with the opening of The Morrison, across the river North Side is coming into its own.

On Lower Ormond Quay across from the Millennium Bridge, the hotel's eclectic exterior combines the facade of a former Georgian townhouse with a modern stone and glass front. The oh-so-stylish interiors were largely influenced by consultant John Rocha and mix clean lines, natural materials and a palette of neutrals accented with crimson red.

Accommodations comprise 84 bedrooms, six suites and a fabulous penthouse with arguably one of the best views of the city. Similarly sharp decor is found within, softened by crisp linens, deep-pile carpets and velvet Rocha-designed throws. All rooms feature the latest technological amenities and many overlook the River Liffey.

'Halo' restaurant is celebrated for its European cuisine served in a dramatic atrium setting. Night owls will also enjoy 'Lobo' and after-hours bar (under the watchful gaze of a 15-foot Africanesque head).

Add to this sleek, professional service and a reliably sophisticated clientele - it's only logical that The Morrison was recently named one of *Conde Nast Traveller's* 'Top 40 Hot Spots'.

dromolandcastle

It's been said that there's nothing new under the sun, but Dromoland Castle comes close to disproving it.

Finished in 1828, the construction of this Gothic masterpiece took quite a long time; its history stretches back to before the Battle of Hastings in 1066.

Nestled in the heart of a 300-acre park, the castle became a hotel in 1962 and offers beautifully decorated rooms and suites with Queen Anne furniture and staggering views of the lake and estate grounds.

The simplicity and elegance of its interior have made Dromoland a favourite destination of many of the famous. Jane Fonda, Ted Turner, Faye Dunaway, Cary Grant and Robert Redford are among the numerous celebrities who have stayed here.

Royalty, too, have enjoyed tea and cocktails while admiring portraits of the O'Briens, direct descendants of High King Brian Boru from the early eleventh century. Furthermore, over the past thirty years, Dromoland Estate has developed a reputation as one of the finest golfing venues in the west of Ireland.

For the Irish and for the rest of us, this hotel is a magnificent landmark amid the romantic countryside of a famously beautiful county.

facts
County Clare
T 353 61 368 144
F 353 61 363 355
58 rooms and 17 suites.
Singles/Doubles: From IE£ 130 to 275
Suites: From IE£ 270 to 500
Tax included. Service charge: 15%
Plan: EP
Airport: 12 Km

dining
The Drawing Room: English and European cuisine, one of the best kitchens in the country.

recreation
Fully equipped gymnasium, 18-hole golf course, tennis court, riding, fishing, archery, clay pigeon shooting, mountain biking, hunting and billiards.

additional
Room service. Helipad.
Music concerts.
Sauna. Steam rooms.
Aromatherapy. Reflexology.

kildarehotel

acts
County Kildare
353 1 601 7200
353 1 601 7299
6 rooms and suites.
ingles/Doubles: From IE£ 280 to 350
uites: From IE£ 450 to 1000
ax and service charge included.
lan: CP
irport: 30 minutes

dining
The Byerley Turk:
French gastronomic cuisine.
The Legends Restaurant:
for an intimate dinner.

recreation
Swimming pool, 18-hole golf course,
indoor and outdoor tennis courts,
health centre, squash court,
fitness centre, riding and trout fishing.

additional
Room service. Helipad.
Beauty salon. Saunas.

n 1991, after three years of renovation, a former private residence became The Kildare, one of the finest hotels in reland. Just 17 miles from Dublin, this nineteenth-century manor stands majestically in the middle of a grand park whose gardens are filled with the most wonderful variety of flowers.

nside, the public areas are overflowing with elegant furnishings and works of art. In the drawing room alone, you vill find paintings from eighteenth-century portraits all the way up to Botero, as well as a magnificent fireplace.

Undoubtedly, one of the main draws of the Kildare is golf. It has managed to host the entire Ryder Cup tournamen n 2005, probably thanks to its superb 18-hole course designed by Arnold Palmer.

Other diversions include treatments in the beauty salon and a fantastic indoor swimming pool lit by an overhanging chandelier. You can also fish for salmon or trout in the River Liffey or simply relax and enjoy the Irish countryside and s incomparable light.

he Kildare hotel is definitely the ideal spot for a weekend.

villad'este

Built in 1568 in typical Renaissance style, this former summer residence of the Cardinal Gallio became a hotel in 1873 and has maintained its charm to the present day. Villa d'Este is more than a hotel, it is a state of mind.

You have the feeling that the owners — who are extremely kind — would like everything to be absolutely perfect, and in this, they certainly succeed. Whether you choose the part of the hotel called the 'Cardinal's Building' or the 'Queen's Pavilion', each bedroom is unique. Period furniture and elegant decor contribute to the warm and welcoming atmosphere that characterise this idyllic place.

If you choose the Cardinal's Building, take a room on the first or second floor so that from your balcony you will have a view of the lake and the countryside. If at all possible book room 133, which has the most beautiful furniture and an especially amazing chandelier.

The Pavilion is recommended for those in search of peace, quiet and more intimate surroundings. Here, all the rooms have a unique view of the lake. The service embodies the image of Villa d'Este: perfect, charming and elegant. It is not only those who love hotels who will appreciate this place; lovers of art and architecture will relish as long a stay as possible.

facts
Via Regina, 40
T 39 031 3481
F 39 031 3488 44
110 rooms and 55 suites.
Singles/Doubles: From ITL 412 500
Suites: From ITL 1 100 000
Tax and service charge included.
Plan: CP
Open March to mid-November.
Airport: 45 minutes

dining
The Veranda and The Grill: traditional Italian cuisine and local specialities.
Kisho: Japanese restaurant.

recreation
Indoor and outdoor swimming pools, tennis courts, squash, fitness centre, windsurfing, sailing and water-skiing, golf simulator, putting-green.
Seven 18-hole golf courses nearby.

additional
24-hour room service. Garage. Boutiques. Beauty salon. Hair Stylist. Night-Club. Piano bar.
Body and facial treatments.
New spa offering beauty treatments. Sauna. Turkish baths. Massage. Hydro-aromatherapy.

facts

Piazza della Repubblica, 7
T 39 055 273 51
F 33 055 273 5888
98 rooms and 9 suites.
Singles/Doubles:
From ITL 510,000 to 1,100,000
Suites: From ITL 1,500,000
Tax and service charge not
included.
Plan: EP
Airport: 20 minutes

dining

L'Incontro: for Italian and Tuscan
specialities.
Bar for cocktails.

recreation

18-hole golf course and tennis courts
nearby.

additional

24-hour room service and concierge.
Meeting and reception facilities.
Same day laundry service.

Florence, one of the world's most beautiful and historical cities, is home to a new and soon to be highly regarded hotel. The Savoy occupies a corner of the Piazza della Republica within easy walking distance of the Duomo, Campanile and Uffizi Gallery. Built in 1893 as the offices of a wealthy banker, the building was eventually turned into an exclusive hotel that counted members of the aristocracy among its privileged guests. A dedicated team of architects and designers recently modernised the property thanks to Sir Rocco Forte, also reviving the elegance that was the hallmark of the Savoy in its heyday.

Decorated in subtle tones, rooms and suites convey the sleek sophistication particular to Italian design. Most of them offer views of the Duomo. What's more, conveniences such as fax machines, data ports and personal valet service upon request make this hotel an especially good choice for business travellers.

'L'Incontro' opens onto the square during good weather for open-air dining. Here, not only will you savour outstanding regional cuisine, but also the sights and sounds of the city as you dine in the warm Florentine sunshine and watch the world pass by. Finally, the charming staff provide an extremely high level of service, making each stay an experience that demands to be repeated.

grandhotel

Grand is the word, indeed.

The distinguished five-story Grand Hotel Florence faces a small piazza alongside the city's River Arno. Formerly a nineteenth-century palace, during the early 1900s the building was transformed into a hotel fit for a king.

The Grand's public areas are decorated in sumptuous Renaissance style and overflow with gorgeous antiques and works of art. An impressive marble-floored winter garden/lounge topped by a stained glass ceiling is the centerpiece — a wonderful place to spend a peaceful few moments, if not the whole afternoon.

The guest roomrs feature all the amenities you would expect from a cosmopolitan property of this calibre. Whether you choose one in the imperial or Florentine style, you will encounter frescoes, fine silks and brocades and lavish bathrooms (with lovely marble tubs for hot baths after a long day of sightseeing). A few have balconies overlooking the Arno, while others have views of the Piazza Ognissanti or the Ponte Vecchio. The lovely 'Incanto' restaurant serves italian cuisine with Tuscan flavours at lunch and dinner, overseen by an endearing staff who will treat you like royalty.

facts
Piazza Ognissanti, 1
T 39 055 288 781
F 39 055 217 400
107 rooms and suites.
Singles/Doubles:
From ITL 655 000 to 1 194 000
Suites:
From ITL 1 600 000 to 4 300 000
Tax and service charge included.
Plan: EP
Airport: 8 Km

dining
Incanto: Italian cuisine with regional Tuscan flavours.

recreation
18-hole golf course, health club and tennis courts nearby.

additional
24-hour room service. Concierge. Banquet and meeting facilities. Business center. Multilingual staff. Massage on request.

villasanmichele

facts

Via di Doccia, 4
T 39 055 5678 200
F 39 055 5678 250
22 rooms and 15 suites.
Singles/Doubles: From ITL 810 000
Suites: From ITL 2 600 000
Open March through December.
Airport: 10 Km

dining

Restaurant in the loggia with a
terrace and unbroken view of
Florence.
Indoor restaurant in the Cloister.
Piano Bar.

recreation

A unique 85-foot heated outdoor
swimming pool overlooking
ancient Florence and small
gymnasium by the pool.
18-hole golf courses, tennis courts
and riding nearby.

additional

24-hour room service.
Courtesy scheduled shuttles
to Florence.
Meeting rooms.
Banquet facilities.

One of the great advantages of the Villa San Michele is its location. It's away from the noise and bustle of Florence (a real benefit during the height of summer, when the city can be packed with tourists), and is in Fiesole, arguably the most beautiful Tuscan town near the region's capital.

It's not easy to describe the sheer beauty of this listed historic building. Perhaps we can only quote Paul Valéry's remark that 'God is in the details' to describe the intense charm of the place.

The Michelangelo façade sets the tone, and beyond that, the frescoes, patios and indoor courtyards create a feeling of immense peace and calm. Skillful renovation of some of the building's architectural features, such as a chapel now serving as the lobby and reception area, add to the unique atmosphere. Another former chapel hidden in the lemon tree and flower-filled gardens houses a private double-roomed suite that has got to be one of the most perfect honeymooning spots anywhere.

Exquisite Italian specialities are served in The Cloister and The Cenacolo — the former a glass-enclosed ancient courtyard, the latter what used to be the refectory. And do set aside a lunch or dinner for the open-air Loggia, offering more informal cuisine and outstanding views of the Arno Valley.

La Posta Vecchia, a sixteenth-century post house that was once the former summer residence of John Paul Getty, is above all a magnet for art lovers. It is here that the American billionaire, with the help of 'l'Occhio' Federico Zeri, the famous art historian, accumulated his treasures, ceramics, Raphael school Gobelins tapestries and paintings.

The pleasure of admiring them can today be shared by the privileged few staying in the twelve bedrooms and seven suites of this gem of a hotel near Rome.

Each room is different (the Medici suite being the most beautiful) and the stunning sixteenth and seventeenth-century furniture make an interesting contrast with satellite television and state-of-the-art telecommunications.

The meals are remarkable for their elegance and style, and guests are expected to dress accordingly: jacket and tie are strongly advised.

The sumptuous indoor swimming pool is an unforgettable experience — classical music is played while you paddle!

In addition to all this, the place is overflowing with history. It is said that a villa belonging to Julius Caesar lies underneath. Now, what other hotel can say *that*?

facts
Palo Laziale
T 39 06 994 9501
F 39 06 994 9507
12 rooms and 7 suites.
Singles/Doubles: From ITL 775 000
Suites: From ITL 1 600 000
Tax and service charge included.
Plan: EP
Airport: 20 km

dining
The restaurant serves exquisite Italian cuisine.

recreation
Swimming pool, tennis courts and riding.
18-hole golf course nearby.

additional
Sauna. Excursions. Beach. Helipad. Limousine airport transfer.

facts
Costa Smeralda
T 39 0789 977 111
F 39 0789 976 617
123 rooms and suites.
Singles/Doubles:
From ITL 1 030 000 to 2 800 000
Tax: 10%.
Plan: FAP
Open from March to November.
Airport: 40 minutes

dining
Cala di Volpe restaurant serves
international cuisine.
Il Pontile: bar and live piano bar.

Barbecue pool restaurant for
Mediterranean buffet lunch.
Pool bar.

recreation
Salt water swimming pool,
fitness centre, tennis court, putting
green, windsurfing, jet skiing and
water skiing.
18-hole golf course nearby.

additional
Room service. Concierge. Hair stylist.
Meeting facilities. Fully air-conditioned.
Boutiques. Bridge room.
Private beach and harbour.

The five star hotel Cala di Volpe in prestigious Costa Smeralda is a hotel like no other.
2001 will see a new Cala di Volpe after a major renovation plan has been completed. With its own private beach, the hotel is more like an entire Mediterranean fishing village tumbling in the sea. The new air-conditioned bedrooms featuring brand new bathrooms are decorated in shades of white and soberly furnished: all of them boast superb views thanks to different terraces surrounding them.
Cala di Volpe is a hotel to recommend in particular to travellers who want to stay away from the crowds: the Costa Smeralda is packed with tourists in summer. Here, you can enjoy all the advantages of an exclusive village thanks to attentive, discreet and professional service.
Three sisters hotels are also located in the area offering an alternative with the same combination of high quality and top standard of service.
The marina of Porto Cervo, where the Aga Khan has built the most luxurious yacht club in the world, is not far away. Look out for your budget (which will already have been well-dented) because it's one of the most expensive places anywhere.

Tucked into a hillside above Portofino's tiny bay, the Hotel Splendido is a sixteenth-century former Benedictine monastery that opened as a hotel in 1901. One of the most beautiful on the Italian Riviera, It has long been loved by a famous clientele.

A graceful pink and white exterior hints at what you will find inside. Tasteful furniture, Carrara marble and a variety of frescoes, create an authentic Mediterranean atmosphere. Bedrooms feature parquet floors, walls embellished with trompe l'oeil murals and the bathrooms are well-appointed.

The views (which include the occasional ocean-liner anchored nearby) will vie with the cuisine for your attention when dining on the terrace, and even from the seawater swimming pool you can take in remarkable scenery through the palms and pines.

All the staff are friendly and professional, but Guest Relations Fausto Allegri deserves special mention: to say that he is well-connected is putting it mildly.

In 1998, the grand dame of Portofino welcomed a little sister. Overlooking the piazzetta and waterfront, the sixteen-room Splendido Mare occupies what was the village's first hotel. Completely renovated to match the sophistication of the Splendido, it offers an intimate alternative, indoor/outdoor gourmet dining at the Chuflay Bar Restaurant and of course, access to all the facilities up the hill.

facts
Viale Baretta, 13
T 39 0185 267 801
F 39 0185 267 806
41 rooms and 27 suites.
Singles/Doubles:
From ITL 780 000
Suites: From ITL 2 350 000
Tax and service charge included.
Plan: EP
Airport: 40 km

dining
La Terrazza: regional cuisine
Swimming pool restaurant for every day meals.
Piano Bar.

recreation
Heated seawater swimming pool, tennis court and fitness centre.
18-hole golf course and water sports nearby.

additional
Meeting rooms. Banquet facilities.
24-hour room service.
Business secretarial services.
Boutiques. Beauty salon.
Hair stylist. Sauna. Babysitting.
Private boat for excursions.

www.splendido.orient-express.com

hasslervillamedici

Situated high on the famous Piazza di Spagna, the Hassler Villa Medici is a rare example of an establishment whose reputation pales in comparison to what one actually finds.

Run by Roberto Wirth, descendant of a great family of hoteliers, the Hassler achieves an unusual but effective balance between Louis XVI-era style and contemporary design.

The bedrooms are enchanting and thoroughly comfortable, if a bit small. Some have been enlarged after recent renovation, however, and all offer gorgeous views over the Basilica San Pietro and the Trinita dei Monti church.

Though all of the suites are impressive, some deserve particular mention.The San Pietro on the sixth floor guarantees you space, a large terrace and an exceptional view of the Eternal City. The seventh-floor penthouse suite is perhaps even more beautiful and is large enough to throw a party in, should you feel like sharing your good fortune.

The service is prompt and attentive and the staff impeccable, notably concierge Nino Maffezzoni, who is a mine of information about Rome and all its secrets.

A final recommendation: if pasta is your passion, then try 'Alberto Ciarla' and 'Piperno', both in the city.

facts
Trinita dei Monti, 6
T 39 06 699 340
F 39 06 678 9991
85 rooms and 15 suites.
Singles/Doubles:
From ITL 540 000 to 860 000
Tax and service charge included.
Plan: EP
Airport: 45 minutes

dining
The very good restaurant on the roof has a magnificent view over the city.
Salone Eva: for tea.

recreation
Most sporting facilities are available nearby.

additional
Meeting and banqueting rooms. Fully air-conditioned. Beauty salon. Limousine airport transfer on request.

hotelderussie

facts
Via del Babuino, 9
T 39 06 32 8881
F 39 06 32 8888 88
102 rooms and 27 suites.
Singles/Doubles:
From ITL 680,000 to 1,250,000
Suites: From ITL 1,500,000
Tax and service charge not
included.
Plan: EP
Airport: 30 minutes

dining
Le Jardin du Russie: for Italian
specialties.

Stravinskij bar for brunch and
cocktails.

recreation
Health centre with hydrotherapy.
18-hole golf courses and tennis
courts nearby.

additional
24-hour room service and concierge.
Meeting and conference facilities.
Same day laundry service.
Fully equipped spa for turkish baths,
sauna and massage.
Air-conditioning.

Situated on Rome's fashionable Via del Babuino, the Hotel de Russie is an old — and new — landmark of the Eternal City. Designed by famous architect Giuseppe Valadier, the hotel's decidedly non-Italian name comes from the fact that it was a favourite of Russian dignitaries during the 1800s. After changing hands a few times, the building was requisitioned by the Italian military during the Second World War. Next it became the headquarters of Italian state television, only to reopen again at the beginning of this millennium as an exceptional place to stay.

Indisputably, the Hotel de Russie's focal point is its spectacular terraced garden. An oasis of palm trees, transplanted Roman ruins and grottoes, it dates back to the original hotel's inauguration and is one of the best places in Rome to escape the hustle and bustle of the city.

The brand-new rooms are skilfully decorated in serene, dusky tones. Spacious yet cosy, they feature the latest in modern technology.

The service? *Perfetto.* After your arrival, while you're out exploring the Spanish Steps or Piazza del Popolo — both just minutes away — your luggage will be unpacked and your clothes pressed. Truly first class.

High in Italy's rugged Dolomites, the Rosa Alpina is truly a breath of fresh air — and a lot more.

The green and white exterior of this family-run chalet reflects the meadows and snowscapes of the surrounding mountains. Inside it is a Tyrolean-style lodge par excellence, resplendent with glowing timber and seventeenth and nineteenth century furniture.

In the guest rooms, light-coloured linens, wood and marble provide a wholesome and elegant feel. Thoroughly cozy, you might not end up spending too much in them though, for there is plenty waiting outdoors.

Alpine skiing in winter and golf in summer are two main attractions of the surrounding Alta Badia area. As you might expect, the trekking is sublime, and the most adventurous will find paragliding and rock climbing not far away.

In any weather, Rosa Alpina is best known for its health and beauty spa. Modelled after a classic beauty farm, it follows a strictly hands-on approach; modern gym equipment is kept to a minimum in favour of good, old-fashioned massages, baths, aromatherapy, and all-natural products designed to bring out your best.

After a day on the slopes, the green or on the massage table, you'll find further stimulation in 'St. Hubertus', the hotel's intimate restaurant. Here, chef Norbert Niederkofler uses his international experience to create fabulous dishes you're not likely to forget .

facts
Str. Micura de Ru 20
T 39 0471 84 95 00
F 39 0471 84 93 77
31 rooms and 20 suites
Singles/Doubles: From ITL 400,000
Suites: From ITL 600,000 to 1,200,000
Plan: CP
Closed from Easter to mid-June
and from October to November.
Tax & Service charge included.
Airport: 180 km

dining
The three restaurants serve excellent regional cuisine and boast a superb wine list.
Two piano bars.

recreation
Fitness centre, mountain-biking, horseback riding, skiing, hunting, fishing and sailing.
9-hole golf course nearby and skiing in the largest ski area of the world.

additional
Whirlpool. Sauna. Hammam. Solarium. Spa.

facts
34, Piazza Tasso
T 39 081 807 1044
F 39 081 877 1206
93 rooms and 14 suites
Singles/Doubles:
From ITL 390,000 to 2,940,000
Plan: EP
Tax included.
Airport: 30 minutes

dining
Vittoria dining room and the open-air
Bosquet terrace serve traditional
Neapolitan cuisine.

recreation
Outdoor swimming pool.
18-hole golf course nearby.

additional
Conference and meeting room
facilities. Business Centre.
Hairdresser. Massage.
Laundry service. Pets allowed.

High on a clifftop overlooking the Bay of Naples, Sorrento's Grand Hotel Excelsior Vittoria reigns supreme as one of the finest and most unique hotels in Italy. This Belle Époque treasure has been owned and operated by the same family since its opening in 1834. The years in between have seen a stellar roster of guests that include royalty, famous artists and Hollywood beauties — in the 50s, that mysterious woman in the silk scarf and sunglasses might easily have been Sophia Loren or Marilyn Monroe!
Inside, frescoed ceilings, glittering chandeliers and an abundance of antiques evoke a feeling of turn-of-the-century glamour.
Outside, five acres of fragrant orange groves guarantee quiet and provide an idyllic setting for the immense swimming pool.
The aristocratic ambience extends to the rooms and suites, almost all of which have balconies overlooking the bay or gardens.
Particularly special is the Enrico Caruso Suite, which remains in the same style as when the great tenor spent a month there in 1921.
Outstanding Neapolitan haute cuisine is served in the opulent dining room. In summer, once-a-week candlelight buffets are served on the terrace, accompanied by a band for dancing.
And when you're ready for sightseeing, a guests-only lift takes you down to the port, where you can take the public hydrofoil to Capri (just 20 minutes away), Ischia, Naples and, in summer, to the Amalfi Coast.

grittipalace

Built in the sixteenth century by the Doge Andrea Gritti, the Gritti Palace well deserves its name. This magnificent palazzo, situated five minutes from Venice's Piazza San Marco and various museums, allows you to travel back in time without leaving the comfort of the hotel.

From Herbert Von Karajan to Woody Allen (scenes from 'Everyone Says I Love You' were filmed here), very few who have experienced this extraordinary establishment have been unaffected by it. Ernest Hemingway himself never missed an opportunity to stay in the best suite on his every visit to Venice. That is not to say that the Gritti Palace is a snobbish hotel — here, every single guest is considered a VIP.

The air-conditioned rooms are spacious, but ask for one with a view over the canal — the best is number 210 — for some of the others are a bit less beautiful.

Relaxing with a drink on the terrace is a wonderful experience, but as you will have guessed, nothing comes cheap. Outside, don't miss a visit to 'Harry's Bar', where you can lunch and dine as nowhere else in the world. Birthplace of the famous prosecco and white peach Bellini cocktail, the restaurant's carpaccio and risottos are to die for.

facts
Campo S.Maria del Giglio
T 39 041 794 611
F 39 041 520 0942
82 rooms and 9 suites.
Singles/Doubles:
From ITL 606 000 to 1 100 000
Suites: From ITL 2 080 000
Tax and service charge: 10%
Plan: EP
Airport: 30 minutes

dining
Le Club del Doge: gastronomic cuisine with piano bar.
The Longhi Bar: for cocktails and snacks.

recreation
18-hole golf course, tennis courts, swimming pool, windsurfing, water-skiing and sailing nearby.

additional
Concierge. Room service.
Car and boat rental.

Facts

Giudecca, 10
T 39 041 520 7744
F 39 041 520 3930
57 rooms and 52 suites.
Singles/Doubles: From ITL 1 470 000
Suites: From ITL 2 250 000
Tax and service charge included.
Plan: CP
Open from March to November.
Airport: 40 minutes

dining

Le Cipriani: for exceptional
Italian cuisine.
Al fresco restaurant on the terrace.

American Bar and buffet by the pool.
Cip's: pizzeria, grill and 'Dolci' on the
terrace.

recreation

Sea-water heated swimming pool,
tennis court and health club.

additional

Meeting rooms. 24-hour room service.
Business secretarial services.
Boutiques. Hair stylist. Babysitting.
Sauna. Massage. Solarium.
Cooking school. Private harbour.
Private motor launch to and from
Piazza San Marco.

Charles Dickens once said, 'Whatever you hear about Venice will never come up to the reality'. The reality of the Cipriani is that it is a hotel of ubiquitous beauty with an unequalled view over 'La Serenissima'.

As far as the bedrooms are concerned, all are simple, elegant and overlook the lagoon, gardens or the church of San Giorgio Maggiore. Those with views of the swimming pool are highly prized.

Speaking of the (Olympic-sized) pool, it is said that its designer misunderstood the owner and confused feet with metres! The result is easily one of the most impressive sights in a city in which space is at premium.

The 'Palazzo Vendramin' annex, in a completely renovated 15th-century building, boasts nothing less than one butler per bedroom and unrestricted views of Piazza San Marco across the canal. It is also worth considering staying in one of the nine apartments in this part of the hotel, which are truly exceptional. Since 1998, the Cipriani's guests have also been able to enjoy the discreet luxury of the 'Palazzetto', a new annex with five extraordinary suites.

If you are in search of a good restaurant in town, you will find that 'La Furatola' has the most superb seafood and competes with 'Casin Dei Nobili' for the title of best in Venice.

xarapalace

A.D. 1550

Once the ancient capital of Malta, Mdina is a medieval fortress city full of history and culture. It has changed little over the centuries. Inextricably linked to Mdina's history — its walls form part of the bastions — is the Xara Palace. Originally the residence of a noble family, it became a hotel in 1949 and was acquired by the Zammit Tabona family in 1995, with an eye to returning it to its original 17th century glory.

Now brought up to the highest international standards, this historic palazzo is one of the most luxurious establishments in the Maltese islands. Experts have used drawings from historical archives to restore the building as accurately as possible, with magnificent results.

As a guest, you will stay in one of 17 individually designed luxury suites. Some have been taken back to their original six-metre height, and now include a mezzanine. Like the rest of the hotel, their decor is opulent but not overwhelming, accentuated with antique furniture and original works of art.

The rooftop De Mondion restaurant is one of Malta's gastronomic treasures. The Trattoria offers lighter meals, and cocktails may be enjoyed in the glass-topped atrium bar.

facts
Misrah Il-Kunsill
T 356 450 560
F 356 452 612
17 suites.
Singles/Doubles: From MTL 95 to 150
Tax included.
Plan: EP
Airport: 8 km

dining
De Mondion, the roof-top restaurant, provides the finest seasonal produce to create subtle northern Italian and richer Mediterranean dishes.

Tratorria: for snacks and drinks.
The Atrium Bar: for aperitifs and cocktails.

recreation
18-hole golf course, tennis courts, hiking, horseback riding, fishing and sailing at the nearby Marsa Sports Club.

additional
Room service. Conference facilities. Secretarial services. Private dining room available on request. Beauty center with a sauna.

Veuve Clicquot

LA GRANDE DAME

hoteldeparis

Made famous the world over by its royal family, Monaco is equally celebrated for the luxury hotels it hosts.

Those who love to be pampered, who adore formal surroundings and the ultimate in luxury will find their dreams fulfilled at the Hotel de Paris. By far and away the best hotel in Monte Carlo, it is grandeur itself.

Built a little after the Casino in 1864 — it is impossible to leave the principality without placing your bets on the green baize — everything here exudes quality, starting with the beautiful lobby, whose magnificent walls, ceilings and chandeliers vie for attention.

The same opulence extends to the bedrooms, which offer breathtaking panoramic views of the Mediterranean.

It goes without saying that the service and the cuisine are beyond reproach; Alain Ducasse, award-winning chef at the marvellous Louis XV restaurant, is surely responsible for its indisputable success.

Although the hotel lacks its own beach, there is complementary shuttle service throughout the day to the 'Monte Carlo Beach Hotel', just five minutes away.

A new restaurant in town? 'Quai des Artistes' has a great harbour view and a menu emphasing Mediterranean cuisine.

facts
Place du Casino
T 377 9216 3000
F 377 9216 3850
141 rooms and 53 suites.
Singles/Doubles: From FRF 2310
Suites: From FRF 3500 to 4800
Tax and service charge included.
Plan: EP
Airport: 25 km

dining
Le Louis XV: for Mediterranean haute cuisine.
Le Grill: for lunch and dinner on the roof.

La Terrasse de la Salle Empire: for romantic dining.
Le Coté Jardin: for informal lunches

recreation
Swimming pool and fitness centre at 'Les Thermes Marins'.
18-hole golf course and tennis nearby

additional
Meeting rooms. Boutiques.
Hair stylist. The spa 'Les Thermes Marins' with two swimming pools, fitness centre, Turkish bath and sauna. Casino and helipad nearby

facts
Square Beaumarchais
T 377 92 16 40 00
F 377 92 16 38 52
227 rooms and suites.
Singles/Doubles:
From FRF 1710 to 3120
Tax and service charge included
Plan: EP
Airport: 25 km

dining
Vistamar restaurant for fresh seafood.
Bar.

recreation
Swimming pool and fitness centre
at 'Les Thermes Marins'.
18-hole golf course and tennis nearby.

additional
Room service. Concierge.
Beauty salon. Parking.
Meeting and banquet facilities.

Built in the early 1900's, the Hotel Hermitage's opulent, aristocratic air stops just short of decadence.
One of the great hotels of the Belle Époque, it has retained its high standards and is today as elite and esteemed as ever.
Evidence that you are in a true palace is everywhere, from the coffered ceilings with their intricate mouldings to the elaborate mosaic floors.
The exquisite winter garden, topped by an art nouveau stained glass dome, was designed by none other than Gustave Eiffel himself.
The rooms, with high ceilings and tall French windows overlooking the Grimaldi Palace, are spacious and enjoy a subtle glamour thanks to harmonious colour schemes and brass beds. If you can get one with a balcony, the view of the harbour or coastline is especially grand.
Finally, the Hermitage is privileged to have as its chef the talented Joel Garault, whose innovative, exquisite creations have brought the aptly-named Salle Belle Epoque much acclaim of late. His success in this magnificent dining room has led to the recent opening of a second restaurant, Vistamar, dedicated to the finest in local seafood.

gleneagles

It would be a shame to go to Gleneagles without golf clubs.

Only one hour from Edinburgh and from Glasgow, this resort was truly made for golfers, with three spectacular courses (Monarch's, designed by Jack Nicklaus, is wonderful). For riders too: the equestrian centre is among the best in the world. The rooms are traditional, spacious and charming — if a little old-fashioned — with very British furniture and views of the countryside or tennis courts. The best can be found in the front part of the hotel; among them, you should try to reserve suite 210 or 212 for their views of the valley.

From your first wholehearted Scottish welcome you will be looked after warmly and well by the friendly and helpful staff. However, silence is respected also and no one will disturb you during afternoon tea, that's for certain!

This hotel, recently judged to be the best in the country, was where the late King Hussein of Jordan and his wife spent their honeymoon.

Evenings can be cold in Scotland, so either bring warm clothing or — better yet — go shopping at the hotel's boutiques which sell marvellous cashmere at very reasonable prices.

facts
Perthshire
T 44 1764 662 231
F 44 1764 662 134
229 rooms and suites.
Singles/Doubles: From GB£ 165
Suites: From GB£ 555 to 1350
Tax included.
Plan: CP
Airport: 75 km

dining
Three restaurants serve very fine cuisine.

recreation
Three 18-hole and one 9-hole golf courses, Golf Academy, five tennis courts, riding, fishing, gymnasium, shooting and falconry school.

additional
24-hour room service.
Sophisticated conference room.
Limousine service.
Shopping arcade.
Spa. Jacuzzis. Helipad.

acts
One Devonshire Gardens
44 141 339 2001
44 141 337 1663
7 rooms and suites
ngles/Doubles:
om GB£ 145 to 230
an: EP
irport: 15 minutes

dining
The restaurant serves fine
international cuisine in elegant
surroundings.

recreation
Health centre, tennis courts
and 18-hole golf course nearby.

additional
Meeting facilities.
Room service.

Only ten minutes from the centre of Glasgow and in the heart of the West End, three adjoining terrace houses form One Devonshire Gardens, a charming hotel opened in 1986 by Ken MacCulloch, a hotelier of international repute.

Described by the late Leonard Bornstein as 'pure theatre', the hotel's baroque interior smoulders with deep colours that make a striking contrast with the classical exterior, not to mention the less-than-balmy Scottish weather!

'One Devon' has already welcomed a large and eclectic mix of guests, among them many musicians. David Bowie and Eric Clapton, as well as actors Michael Keaton, Pierce Brosnan and Emma Thompson have recently paid a visit.

Each of the bedrooms have their own style, so it's tricky to highlight one in particular. However, a wise choice would be Room 9, with its four-poster bed in shades of black and cream, beautiful fireplace and stunning marble bathroom.

The hotel's Michelin-starred restaurant is undoubtedly one of the best in Glasgow. Credit for this goes to chef Andrew Farlie, whose inspired creations excite both the palate and the eye.

To sum up, One Devonshire Gardens should be at the top of your list if you are planning a trip to Scotland's cultural capital, and is all the more attractive for its very reasonable prices, a truly rare phenomenon among first-class hotels.

Barcelona is one of the most dynamic cities in Europe. This is largely a consequence of its successful 1980s programme of urban regeneration, which not only restored countless buildings and public squares to their former glory, but also resulted in the city's highly-praised staging of the Olympic games in 1992.

Now Barcelona has been chosen by the prestigious Ritz-Carlton group to host its first European hotel on the Mediterranean. Ideally situated beside the sea, the Hotel Arts takes the form of a tower with a surprisingly modern, white metal framework design. Dominating the Olympic port and the new marina, the hotel's incomparable and novel style is characterized by cascading water in the lobby, a beautiful collection of contemporary art in the public rooms and very modern interiors in understated colours. The building is more than forty storeys high, providing superb views of the sea, the city, the Tibidabo mountains and the enormous and futuristic Frank Gehry goldfish sculpture outside the entrance.

All the rooms are more than comfortable, but by reserving one on the thirtieth to thirty-third floors, you'll be assured of spectacular views — and perhaps vertigo.

Finally, in town, don't miss a visit to 'Tenorio' for its wonderful Catalan cuisine.

facts
Carrer de la Marina 19-21
T 34 9 3221 1000
F 34 9 3221 3045
455 rooms and suites.
Singles/Doubles: From ESP 45 000
Plan: EP
Airport: 20 minutes

dining
Café Veranda: Catalonian
and Mediterranean cuisine.
The Newport Room: for innovative
Mediterranean dishes.
Goyescas: for traditional Spanish tapas.
The Salo: for tea.

recreation
Outdoor swimming pool and fitness
centre.
18-hole golf course, tennis courts
and water sports nearby.

additional
Conference and banqueting
facilities. Concierge. Business centre.
24-hour room service. Sauna.
Massage. Jacuzzis. Babysitting.
Beauty salon.

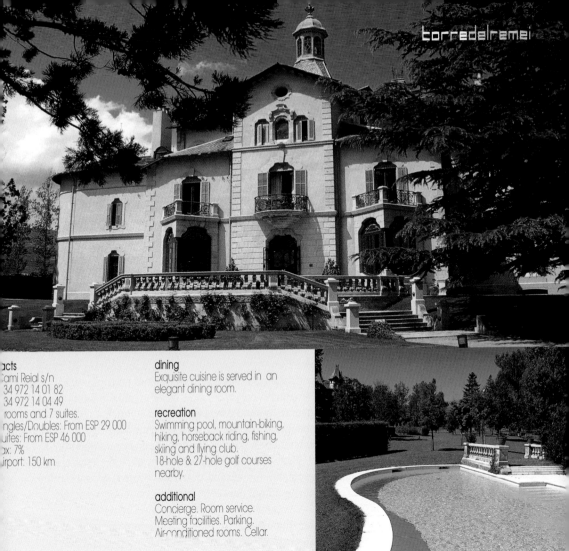

acts
Cami Reial s/n
34 972 14 01 82
34 972 14 04 49
rooms and 7 suites.
ngles/Doubles: From ESP 29 000
uites: From ESP 46 000
ax: 7%
irport: 150 km

dining
Exquisite cuisine is served in an elegant dining room.

recreation
Swimming pool, mountain-biking, hiking, horseback riding, fishing, skiing and flying club.
18-hole & 27-hole golf courses nearby.

additional
Concierge. Room service. Meeting facilities. Parking. Air-conditioned rooms. Cellar.

Originally a private residence built in 1910, then confiscated and used as a school and hospital during the Spanish Civil War, he mansion that houses Torre del Remei was all but deserted when proprietors Josep-Maria and Loles Boix came upon it by chance in the late 1980s. Already owners of one flourishing hotel, they knew a good thing when they saw one.

ubsequent renovation created an establishment that artfully blends past and present, majesty and calm. The original Gaudi poch architecture, characterised by arabesque arches and intricately plastered ceilings, is now offset by walls in cool astels, glowing wooden floors and modernist décor. Eleven bedrooms are each named after geographical features seen om the windows. Beds are large and done up in embroidered linen, bathrooms are huge and feature whirlpool baths. While Senora Boix manages the daily operations and very attentive staff, Josep-Maria is master of the kitchen. His award-vinning, often regional cuisine with ingredients from the hotel's kitchen garden — draws locals as well as tourists to the dining room.

Also restored, the five-acre grounds include the original hundred year-old sequoias and several new ones, making for thirty pecies in all. Here you can enjoy the swimming pool, putting green or restorative strolls around the property.

La Bobadilla is more than a hotel — it's a town unto itself.

Olive groves and almond orchards outside, white walls, tile roofs, lush patios and vaulted passages within, this luxurious estate is a cross between a Moorish village and an Andalusian cortijo, or ranch. At the centre is a sixteenth century-style chapel, whose 1,595-pipe organ is used for weddings and weekend concerts.

'Romantic' does not begin to describe the feeling of this place that seems plucked from the pages of 1001 Arabian Nights. The atmosphere is so tranquil and inviting, usually-shy goldfinches build their nests in the interior courtyard!

Imagination and exquisite good taste are evident in the sixty-two different styles of rooms and suites. Each one is of Spanish inspiration (terra cotta and mahogany being the main design elements) and all have private terraces or gardens.

The semi-formal restaurant, La Finca, cooks with produce from the hotel's garden and meat reared on local farms. A second, El Cortijo, serves more down-to-earth regional cuisine.

And while it's hard to imagine anyone wanting to leave the grounds, La Bobadilla's excellent location means it is possible to visit Andalusia's other famous cities, Málaga, Granada, Cordoba and Seville, within the course of a day.

facts
Finca la bobadilla, P.O Box 144
T 34 958 321 861
F 34 958 321 810
53 rooms and 9 suites.
Singles/Doubles :
From ESP 36 900 to 54 400
Suites: From ESP 62 600 to 122 100
Tax: 7%
Plan: CP
Airport: 70 Km

dining
La Finca : for international and gourmet cuisine.
El Cortijo : for Spanish food.

recreation
Outdoor swimming pool,
indoor heated swimming pool,
tennis court, fitness centre,
horseback riding, archery,
mountainbikes, quad-bikes,
table tennis and clay shooting.

additional
Meeting rooms. Boutiques.
Beauty salon.
Saunas. Massage.
Turkish baths.
Jacuzzis. Concerts.

facts
La Boladilla Baja
Ctra. Cadiz, Km. 163.5
T 34 95 2794345
F 34 95 2794825
73 rooms and suites.
Singles/Doubles:
From ESP 36,000 to 269,000
Plan: EP
Airport: 50 minutes

dining
Lido restaurant offers high-class
Mediterranean cuisine.
Piano Bar and Bistro Felix for haute
european cuisine with asiatic flavours.

recreation
Swimming pool, water sports
and fitness centre.
27-hole golf course nearby.

additional
24-hour room service. Concierge.
Private butler service on request.
Rolls-Royce limousine and luxury car
rental service. Valet parking.
Boutiques. Business facilities.
Beach club. Health Clinic and Spa.
Massage. Beauty treatments.
Jacuzzi. Sauna.

Opened in 1996, Las Dunas has already established a reputation as one of the finest resorts in Southern Spain.
With sub-tropical gardens, fountains, and a 20-metre pool, this sprawling pink hacienda was constructed in the regional style with Moorish touches. Its privileged position on the Costa del Sol guarantees excellent climate and memorable views. In the rooms and suites, vibrant and pastel colours mix throughout the fabrics and furnishings to create a stimulating yet restful ambience. The spacious bathrooms feature traditional Andalucian tiling and extra-large tubs.

Restaurante Lido is a favourite even with locals, who come for the superb food and sumptuous surroundings. Centred on an octagonal room with a magnificent crystal chandelier and trompe-l'oeil walls, the menu features healthy Mediterranean cuisine (with organic produce from the hotel's own farm) and an impressive ten-page wine list. There is also Piano Bar & Bistro Felix for light, Euro-Asian dishes and nightly live music.

Besides a high-tech fitness room and excellent spa, La Dunas offers two facilities rarely found elsewhere. The Regena Sol Kur-Clinic's in-house physicians apply traditional and alternative therapies to remedy everything from stress to sports injuries, while 'Dr. Schulte's World of Beauty' offers revolutionary clinical treatments to rejuvenate one's appearance.

Created in 1954 by Prince Alfonso Von Hohenholc, the Marbella Club hosts an international clientele who come back year after year, giving the place the atmosphere of an exclusive club.

On one side of the property are light and spacious rooms with bamboo furniture, brightly-coloured fabrics and private terraces or balconies. On the other are two and three-bedroom bungalows in Andalusian style, some with private swimming pools and Jacuzzis.

In the mornings, the buffet breakfast is served on the patio amid luxuriant gardens. With the birds singing and the sun shining, it's truly a delight. Later you can enjoy the Michelin-starred cuisine of Juan Galvez, which combines the best of Spanish and international flavours.

The new beachfront spa features a dynamic indoor seawater pool, steam baths and 12 private rooms offering thalasso and beauty programs, as well as slimming, rejuvenation or stress relief.

Admittedly, some guests are not keen on numerous tourists in the area. However, if you adopt the Latin attitude to life — *Que sera sera* — you'll have no trouble enjoying yourself in this ideally located hotel right beside the sea.

In town, try to reserve a table in the garden of 'La Meridiana' to sample the best of local cuisine in an equally luscious setting.

facts
Bulevar Príncipe Alfonso von Hohenlohe s/n
T 34 95 282 2211
F 34 95 282 3018
132 rooms and suites.
Singles/Doubles.
From ESP 28,000 to 79,000
Suites: From ESP 49,000
Tax: 7%
Plan: EP
Airport: 35 minutes

dining
Marbella Club Grill Restaurant: for Spanish and international cuisine.
The Winter Garden: for buffet breakfast
The Bach Club Restaurant: for buffet lunch and light meals.
Summer & winter bar.

recreation
Three indoor and outdoor swimming pools, private 10-hole golf course, riding stables and seasonal water sports.
Puente Romano tennis & fitness centre nearby.

additional
Conference room,
24-hour room service.
Dry cleaning and laundry service.
Air conditioning. Boutique gallery.
Baby sitting service on request.
Bilingual secretarial service on request. Currency exchange.
Car rental service.

hotelsonvida

The Spanish island of Mallorca saw a major increase in hotel development after becoming a favoured getaway for the rich and famous during the 1960s. If not all of the new properties have been complete successes, a few manage to stand out. Far and away the best of them is the Hotel Son Vida.

On a pine-covered hilltop surrounded by fourteen hundred acres of sub-tropical park, the hotel inhabits a former thirteenth-century castle with a magnificent view over the stunning bay of Palma.

Since its inauguration in 1961, many distinguished guests have passed through its turreted entrance to enjoy a peaceful, exclusive stay (Prince Rainier of Monaco, the King of Arabia, Emperor Haile Selassie, rock and movie stars too).

Contrasting the medieval atmosphere, each spacious accommodation features air-conditioning, direct-dial phone and satellite television. Superior rooms are situated facing the Bay of Palma and standard rooms have views over the hotel's gardens.

Golfers take note: the Son Vida is equally celebrated for its two exceptional 18-hole courses, the Son Vida and the Sun Muntaner, which are for the exclusive use of guests.

facts
Castillo Son Vida
T 34 971 790 000
F 34 971 790 017
171 rooms and suites.
Singles/Doubles: From ESP 29100
Suites: From ESP 110 000
Tax and service charge not included.
Plan: EP
Airport: 10 Km

dining
Restaurant Bellver:
for international cuisine.
Restaurant Jardin: gourmet restaurant.

Grill restaurant by the swimming-pool.
Bar Armas: Piano bar.

recreation
Outdoor and indoor swimming pool
tennis courts and fitness centre.
Two 18-hole golf courses for hotel
guests only.

additional
Conference and meeting facilities.
24-hour room service. Car rental. Ha
stylist. Activities for children.
Excursions. Massage. Turkish Bath.
Body treatments. Jacuzzi. Sauna.

facts
Mijas Golf
T 34 95 247 3050
F 34 95 247 6783
117 rooms and 27 suites.
Singles/Doubles:
From ESP 35 600 to 65 000
Tax: 7%
Plan: EP
Airport: 32 Km

dining
Le Nailhac: French cuisine.
El Andaluz: for regional
and special dietary menus.

La Fuente: for breakfast and lunch.
Bar Saint Tropez: for cocktails.

recreation
Indoor and outdoor swimming pools,
two 18-hole golf courses and five
tennis courts.

additional
Fully-equipped banqueting and
convention rooms. 24-hour room
service and concierge. Boutiques.
Limousine service. Beauty salon.
Massage. Sauna. Nightclub.
Babysitting. Thalassotherapy centre.

Usually it's unwise to generalise about the effect a hotel has on its guests, but it's fair to say that at the Byblos Andaluz you will...

- Marvel at the harmony of Moorish and European styles
- Relax on your balcony and take in the stunning scenery
- Find it hard to choose between the stylish rooms and the 1,500 square foot suites
- Play golf on two marvellous courses designed by Robert Trent Jones
- Experience one of the most comprehensive spa in Europe
- Luxuriate in the swimming pools and saunas
- Indulge in local and gastronomic cuisine
- Not be surprised to bump into royalty
- Never forget the exquisite and refined ambience
- Urge your friends and neighbours to stay there

hotelAlFonsotrece

Built to host heads of state and other high-ranking guests of the 1929 Great Ibero-American Exhibition, the Hotel Alfonso XIII was designed to be the most luxurious in Europe. Inaugurated by the king himself, today this quirky and charming hotel remains an historical palace whose decor is a mix of Moorish and Art Deco.

The hotel centres around an authentic Spanish courtyard with brick arches, flowering orange trees and a fountain. Its public areas are resplendent with marble floors, wood-panelled ceilings, heavy Moorish lamps, stained glass and ceramic tile in typical Sevillian colours.

Rooms and suites are furnished in either Moorish, Baroque or Castilian style; the former feature elaborate plasterwork, the latter Murano glass chandeliers. All have plenty of wood, gorgeous emerald linen curtains and bathrooms with marble floors. Those overlooking the courtyard are peaceful and attractive, while rooms on the outside have lovely views of the city.

The Royal Suite is the hotel's most opulent, offering expansive living quarters with exclusive services.

The Alfonso's restaurant is one of the best in Seville and highly recommended. However, If you feel like venturing further into town, 'La Taberna del Alabardero' and 'La Albahaca' are two not to miss.

facts
San Fernando, 2
T 34 95 422 28 50
F 34 95 421 50 33
127 rooms and 19 suites.
Singles/Doubles: From ESP 42 500
Suites: From ESP 55 500
Tax: 7%
Plan: EP
Airport: 20 minutes

dining
San Fernando: for a selection of regional and international cuisine.
Kaede: for Japanese specialties.
San Fernando Bar: for cocktails.

recreation
Outdoor swimming pool.
18-hole golf course nearby.

additional
24-hour room service. Concierge.
Laundry and dry-cleaning.
Meeting and banquet facilities.
Butler service. Secretarial services.
Parking. Business centre.
Beauty salon. Car rental.
Excursions.

parkhotel

facts
CH-6363
T 41 41 612 90 10
F 41 41 612 90 11
58 rooms and suites.
Singles/Doubles: From CHF 305
Suites: From CHF 540 to 670
Tax and service charge included.
Plan: EP
Airport: 75 minutes

dining
Le Club: French gourmet restaurant.
Da Tintoretto: Mediterranean restaurant.
Taverne: chalet-style restaurant offering Swiss specialties.

Cozy piano bar and elegant Club Bar with live music.

recreation
Golf, Country & Leisure Club with heated indoor and outdoor pools, fitness room, hotel-owned par 33 golf course and tennis courts. Water sports, paragliding and river rafting nearby.

additional
24-hour room service. Meeting facilities. Beauty parlour. Sauna. Solarium. Massage. Steam bath. Own boat's pier. Funicular railway. Shopping facilities.

Fifteen hundred feet above Lake Lucerne, in the midst of unspoilt nature, is a mini-community known as The Bürgenstock Hotels & Resort. This unique destination features a selection of three hotels: The Palace, The Grand and The Park. While all of them are impressive, it is the latter that undoubtedly takes first place.

Rebuilt in 1991, the Park combines the best of modern Swiss architecture with equally authentic old-world charm.

Natural stone, glass and woodwork are the main elements of the building, whose windows reveal picture-perfect vistas of the Alps and five lakes including Lucerne. The views are no less spectacular from the elegant, contemporary rooms and suites.

'Polyvalence' is a word that prevails here, meaning that while one might take advantage of the hotel's state-of-the-art meeting facilities to conduct business, another may enjoy the Bürgenstock's many recreational offerings, which include a well-being centre, tennis courts, swimming pools and a golf course founded in 1928.

While guests also have access to the resort's four other restaurants, 'Da Tintoretto' in the Park serves gourmet Mediterranean cuisine in a sophisticated indoor/outdoor setting.

gstaadpalace

High above the picturesque village of Gstaad in the Bernese Oberland is a fairy-tale castle known as The Palace Hotel.
Established in 1913 and run for three generations by the Scherz family, The Palace has earned a reputation for discretion and refined hospitality. Warm and welcoming, it is a bastion of great tradition where comfortable interiors are characterised by rustic elegance and roaring open fireplaces.

The bedrooms and suites are charming; spacious yet cosy, all afford magnificent views of the surrounding alpine meadows, Swiss chalets and snow-capped mountain peaks. A new spectacular penthouse was recently added and consits of three bedrooms, a large living room with fireplace and a surrounding terrace with breathtaking views.

In addition to five restaurants offering dishes to suit every palate, the hotel houses an intimate piano bar perfect for reading or relaxation. Gstaad's most sought-after nightclub, GreenGo, can also be found there.

Spa facilities include a beauty centre run by Swiss clinique 'La Prairie', an indoor/outdoor pool, saunas and massage. A gymnasium, squash court and 18-hole golf course compliment the wide range of mountain sports available nearby.

Whether you choose the Palace Hotel for business or a summer or winter getaway, count on a truly memorable experience.

facts
T 41 33 748 5000
F 41 33 748 5001
64 rooms and 38 suites.
Singles/Doubles: From CHF 310
Suites: From CHF 740 to 2210
Tax and service charge included.
Plan: CP
Open from mid-December to March
and from mid-June to mid-September.
Airport: 95 Km

dining
The Restaurant: elegant Swiss cuisine.
La Grande Terrasse: for lunch and dinner.
The Grill serves superb food.
Le Sans Cravate: for informal dining.
La Fromagerie : for typical swiss fare.

recreation
Indoor and outdoor swimming pools,
four tennis courts, squash,
fitness centre, curling, skating,
rafting and hot-air ballooning.
18-hole golf course and riding nearby

additional
Banquet and meeting facilities.
Boutiques. Beauty salon. Night-Club.
Spa. Saunas. Massage. Steam bath.

facts

T 41 21 613 33 33
F 41 21 613 33 34
170 rooms and suites.
Singles/Doubles: From CHF 385
Suites: From CHF 890
Tax and service charge included.
Plan: EP
Airport: 35 minutes

dining

La Rotonde: gourmet French
restaurant.
Le Café Beau Rivage: Parisian
brasserie with a relaxed atmosphere.
Le Grill Piscine offers light meals.

recreation

Indoor and outdoor swimming pool,
two tennis courts, table tennis and
fitness centre.
18-hole golf course nearby.

additional

24-hour room service and concierge.
Meeting and banquet facilities.
Laundry and dry cleaning service.
Turkish bath. Massage.
Steam rooms and sauna. Solarium.
Baby sitting service on request.
Limousine service. Boutiques.
Parking

Standing on ten acres of private gardens beside Lake Geneva, the Beau Rivage Palace exemplifies the extraordinary standard of hospitality long associated with Swiss hotels.

Favoured by the rich, famous and important since the beginning of the century (Nelson Mandela, the Duke and Duchess of Windsor and many others have stayed here), this grand establishment commands dazzling views over the lake and the majestic Swiss Alps.

The bedrooms? Richly appointed with fine fabrics, tapestries and period furniture, they offer the utmost in elegance and comfort. Whether you choose one with a view of the lake or the mountains, all are very impressive.

The suites? Seven were created to be different and unique in style, each one to suit even the most demanding of guests.

The restaurants? Over fifty chefs are responsible for the impeccably prepared meals served throughout the hotel. For excellent French cuisine in a truly regal setting, reserve a table at 'La Rotonde'. The 'Cafe Beau Rivage', modelled after a Parisian brasserie is perfect for those looking to enjoy a more informal meal. It also happens to be one of the hottest spots in town.

widderhotel

In the heart of Zurich, hidden away in a tiny street among restaurants, boutiques and bakers, is a hotel that proves that appearances can be deceptive. For behind a dozen elegant facades from the twelfth to the seventeenth centuries is the surprisingly futuristic Widder.

Inside, there's such a maze of corridors and staircases it would not be difficult to get lost. The owners wanted to keep the imprint and heritage of each of the buildings, so while one contains Biedermeier furniture another is typically baroque.

It's impossible to recommend one bedroom or suite over another when you consider that each represents the style of a different architect such as Le Corbusier, Frank Lloyd Wright, Adolf Loos or Mario Bellini. Nevertheless, all promise utmost comfort in an atmosphere of the highest style.

In town, the 'Kronenhalle' restaurant is a standard-bearer for classic cuisine. Magnificently decorated with works of art by Picasso, Chagall and Matisse, it never disappoints. 'Zunfthaus Zur Waag' is another excellent choice (but you will definitely need a reservation).

facts
Rennweg, 7
T 41 1 224 2526
F 41 1 224 2424
42 rooms and 7 suites.
Singles/Doubles: From CHF 370
Suites: From CHF 780
Plan: EP
Airport: 15 Km

dining
Widder restaurant:
for light Swiss cuisine.
Widder Bar: for cocktails.

recreation
Swimming pools, tennis courts,
health centre and 18-hole golf
courses nearby.

additional
Room service.
Banqueting and meeting facilities.

ciraganpalace

facts
Ciragan Caddesi, 84
T 90 212 258 3377
F 90 212 259 6687
284 rooms and 32 suites.
Singles/Doubles:
From US$ 300 to 750
Suites: From US$ 750 to 7500
Tax: 17% Service charge included.
Plan: EP
Airport: 25 Km

dining
The Laledan: continental cuisine.
The Tugra: Turkish cuisine.
The Bellini: Italian cuisine.

recreation
Outdoor swimming-pool,
heated indoor swimming pool
and fitness centre.

additional
24-hour room service and concierge.
Meeting facilities. Business centre.
Secretarial services. Boutiques.
Sauna. Turkish bath.
Massage. Jacuzzi.
Solarium.

Situated in the European part of Istanbul between the Bosporus and Yildiz Park, the Ciragan Palace is partly comprised of the nineteenth century palace of the last sultan of the Ottoman Empire. It was expanded and opened as a hotel in 1857.

The bedrooms are furnished in European style with an Asian touch, enhanced by rich Ottoman fabrics and antiques. You can choose one in the sultan's former palace or the new wing opposite, but avoid those with modern decor and furniture, as they tend to be less charming. Still, all the rooms are of good size and enjoy dramatic views of the park or river, where dawn is an unforgettable sight.

The antique swimming pool is cleverly situated next to the river and has no surround, creating the illusion that you are swimming in the Bosporus itself.

With excellent and unobtrusive staff and service, every effort is made to ensure that your stay is a complete success. This may be one reason the hotel is so popular with celebrities (the late John Kennedy Jr. chose it for his honeymoon).

Schedule yourself enough time to visit the numerous palaces that line the banks of the Straits. The Dolmabahce, the Yildiz and of course the Topkapi are deservedly among the most popular.

When this guide tells you that one of the latest Four Seasons creations is in a former prison in the heart of old Istanbul, you would be forgiven for harbouring some doubts about staying there.

However, bear in mind that this hotel group unfailingly creates and maintains hotels of the very highest standard.

Perhaps it is also worth saying that the prison couldn't have been too bad, as it was reserved for artists and aristocrats. You might expect that the rooms would be dark; far from it — in fact, all have at least two windows letting in lots of light, not to mention views of minarets, domes and the Blue Mosque.

While all the rooms are superb and different, the best one is 317 with its unforgettable view of the nearby mosque. The bathrooms, with enormous tubs are particularly remarkable, and large enough to keep a whole family of aristocrats captive.

The service is so good you could quite happily be locked in here for years without chance of escape.

In town, try 'Pandeli' restaurant for a magical taste of the Orient or 'Shashibala', a new hotspot whose cuisine is amongst the best in town.

facts
Tevkifhane Sokak No 1
T 90 212 638 8200
F 90 212 638 8210
65 rooms and suites.
Singles/Doubles:
From US$ 290 to 550
Tax: 15%
Plan: EP
Airport: 20 minutes

dining
The hotel restaurant offers
international cuisine.
Bars.

recreation
Fitness centre.

additional
Meeting facilities.
24-hour room service,
business centre and concierge.
Children's activities.

'acts
Yokusbasi Mevkil
T 90 252 313 8130
F 90 252 313 8131
100 rooms and suites.
Singles/Doubles: From US$ 300
Suites: From US$ 430 to 1100
Tax included.
Plan: EP
Airport: 30 minutes

dining
Tuti restaurant serves international cuisine for everyday meals.
The Lounge Bar: for cocktails.

recreation
Swimming pools, squash and fitness centre.
Riding, boating and watersports nearby.

additional
24-hour room service.Turkish Bath.
Meeting facilities. Sauna. Jacuzzi.
Direct dial telephones with data port.

n ancient times, Bodrum was the birthplace of Heredotus and site of the Tomb of King Mausolus, one of the Seven Wonders of he World. Today one of Turkey's loveliest holiday destinations, it is a meeting place for artists, intellectuals and the international elite. Spread across a hilltop above this bohemian village is the Marmara Bodrum. Embellished with domes and pyramid-topped chimneys, inside you will be surprised by avant-garde interiors more commonly found in Miami or L.A. Omnipresent contemporary art and terrazzo floors mimicking Turkish carpets contribute to the modernist surroundings.

The luxury guestrooms have an almost Japanese feel, simply decorated with wood and stone floors, rough-hewn timber chests and platform beds. In the showers, double sheets of glass contain electronic shades that lift to reveal views across the bedroom to the sea.

There is 'Tuti' for fine dining and the Lounge Bar for cocktails, but keep in mind that Bodrum is famous for its cafes, bars and exotic restaurants (not to mention some of Europe's best discos).

With two swimming pools, an ultra-modern fitness centre and authentic hammam, it will be tempting not to come down from the hill. But do, and visit the Museum of Underwater Archaeology, featuring the world's largest collection of shipwreck artefacts.

asia

thestrand

Often compared to Raffles Hotel in Singapore (they had the same architects), The Strand is something of a landmark in Burma.

Built in 1901 on the banks of the Rangoon River, it immediately featured in turn-of-the century tourist guides as 'the best hotel east of Suez' — quite a compliment at a time when the British Empire was at its most prosperous.

Recently renovated to restore it to 1920s style, the hotel's high ceilings, polished hardwood floors, indoor palms and cane and mahogany furniture combine to evoke a sense of nostalgic elegance. Moments inside the door, you will be struck by the colonial atmosphere and warm light that seem to come from another age.

All the rooms offer an exceptional level of comfort and contain furnishings in traditional, indigenous style. Best of all is the Strand suite: it comprises a verandah, drawing room, enormous canopy bed and a marble and mahogany bathroom.

The service is charming and the staff are always delighted to help in any way they can.

Make it a point to visit the National Museum and especially the Sule and Botataung pagodas, both nearby.

facts
92 Strand Road
T 95 1 243 377
F 95 1 289 880
32 suites.
Singles/Doubles:
From US$ 425 to 450
Suites: From US$ 900
Tax: 10%. Service: 10%
Plan: EP
Airport: 20 minutes

dining
Strand Café: for light meals.
Strand Grill: international cuisine.
The Bar & Lobby Lounge:
for cocktails and for tea.

additional
Conference and meeting rooms.
24-hour room service.
Dry-cleaning service.
24-hour business centre.
Boutiques. Library. Massage.
Excursions.

facts
5 Connaught Road
T 852 2522 0111
F 852 2810 6190
486 rooms and 55 suites.
Singles/Doubles:
From HK$ 2950 to 4200
Suites: From HK$ 5500 to 25 000
Tax: 5%. Service charge: 10%
Plan: EP
Airport: 45 minutes

dining
Vong's: French cuisine.
Mandarin Grill: international cuisine.

Man Wah: Cantonese cuisine
in elegant surroundings.
Three bars.

recreation
Indoor swimming pool
and fitness centre.
18-hole golf course and tennis
nearby.

additional
Conference and banqueting
facilities. Business centre.
24-hour concierge and room
service. Boutiques.

Hospitality is an art in Asia

For more than twenty-five years, one of the greatest exponents in this field has been the Mandarin Oriental, regularly classed among the five best hotels in the world.

The Mandarin maintains the loyalty of its clientele by offering an almost unheard-of level of service (two members of staff for every guest). To the Italian concierge, a well-connected figure, nothing is impossible; whether last-minute airline tickets, a private jet or a reservation in the best restaurants, he will arrange it.

Hate packing and unpacking? No problem — the staff will take care of that too.

When it comes to reserving a room, those whose numbers end in 10 or 12 (regardless of the floor) have the best view of the harbour. If your budget extends to a suite (all of which have balconies) three are particularly spectacular: the Mandarin (2402), the Tamar (2403) and the Macau (2418).

All of the hotel's restaurants are considered among Hong Kong's best but in town, the new trendy restaurants are 'Aqua', 'Blue' and 'Alibi' where reservations are a must.

thepeninsula

Opened in December 1928, the Peninsula quickly forged itself an international reputation as the epitome of elegance and luxury. Since then it has never rested on its laurels and continues to uphold its name.

The rooms have a sophisticated style complimented by rich, rare woods and high ceilings, and every technological amenity one could ask for. A totally silent fax machine, satellite television, compact disc and DVD player, global communications broadband internet access — all can be controlled without moving from one's bed.

The best rooms are those of the tower guests for they have views of the harbour and city, which are truly breathtaking.

If your budget stretches that for, try the 'Garden Suite' with its gorgeous drawing room, 24-hour valet service, its own private lift and enormous terrace overlooking the harbour. If you cannot find a parking space for your helicopter, then don't worry: the hotel has its own pad on the roof.

Don't leave Hong Kong without a cocktail or a meal in 'Felix, the Philippe Starck's designed rooftop restaurant or taking tea in the lobby (Darjeeling or Ceylon, naturally) where the Bach concertos seem to make time stand still.

facts
Salisbury Road
T 852 2920 2888
F 852 2722 4170
246 rooms and 54 suites.
Singles/Doubles:
From HK$ 3000 to 4900
Suites: From HK$ 5600 to 39 000
Tax: 3%. Service charge: 10%
Plan: EP
Airport: 45 minutes

dining
Gaddi's: French cuisine.
Chesa: Swiss cuisine.

The Spring Moon: Chinese cuisine.
The Verandah: for casual dining.
Imasa: Japanese restaurant.
Felix: Pacific Rim dishes.

recreation
Swimming pool and fitness centre.

additional
Conference and banqueting facilities. 24-hour room service. Business centre. Boutiques. Rolls-Royce transfers. Helicopter landing pad. Shopping arcade. Spa.

facts
Goner Road – Rajasthan
91 141 64 0101
91 141 64 0202
71 rooms and 14 suites.
Singles/Doubles:
From US$ 310 to 350
Villas: From US$ 650 to 1200
Tax: 16%
Plan: EP
Airport: 30 minutes

dining
The restaurant serves international
and Asian cuisine.
Bar snack and beverage by the pool.

recreation
Swimming pool, two tennis courts
and fitness centre.

additional
24-hour room service. Spa.
Library. Aromatherapy.
Cultural excursions.
Complimentary round-trip airport
or railway station transfers.
Helipad.
Elephant safari.

Designed like a traditional Indian fortress, Rajvilas was in fact built only recently, after three years of work by the best local craftsmen. With a 250 year old Hindu temple at its centre, the complex is characterised by an abundance of waterfalls, swimming pools, gardens, lawns and fountains. In architectural stye, it echoes the pink palaces of nearby Jaipur.
A remarkable variety of rooms is available. Among them, you should try to book above all numbers 216 and 225 which are… tents! You're probably not used to this kind, though — teak floors, air-conditioning, enormous beds and unique baths (an excellent choice for honeymooners).
The spa, undoubtedly the most beautiful in the country, is set in a traditional Indian house called a 'haveli'. It offers the most modern treatments and healthcare, including aromatherapy, traditional massages and Indian relaxation techniques.
The superb cuisine is due to a very inspired chef who successfully combines European influences with indigenous traditions and ingredients. The result is astonishing — all the more so for being in the heart of India.
Finally, the service is excellent — happy, friendly and courteous — which is perhaps not surprising since the 150 staff are the lucky ones among 7000 interviewed.

Get ready for a hotel that meets every superlative.

Resembling a traditional Balinese village on a terraced hill, the Four Seasons at Jimbaran is made up of one hundred and forty-seven thatched roof villas, four restaurants and a reception pavillion reached by golf carts.

In each of the superb hideaways (one of the most beautiful is number 204), you will find two bedrooms, a plunge pool, outdoor sitting room and a private garden from which you can watch the stunning sunsets over Jimbaran Bay.

Each claims an average of 2,200 square feet; they contain marble floors and imposing beds draped with mosquito nets and look out over gardens filled with bougainvillea and tropical plants. In the two Royal villas you will even find a private Jacuzzi and a swimming pool.

But that's not all: the service surpasses anything you have ever seen. Four staff members per guest means that a couple can count on eight superbly-trained staff waiting on them hand and foot 24 hours a day.

The masseuses are absolutely gifted and pamper you with spa treatments based on natural elements such as sea-salt crystals and seaweed.

The Four Seasons is undoubtedly one of the most stylish hotels in the world and its spa one of the finest in the far East.

facts
Jimbaran Bay
T 62 361 701 010
F 62 361 701 020
147 villas.
Villas: From US$ 550
Tax: 11%. Service charge: 10%
Plan: EP
Airport: 15 minutes

dining
Four restaurants serve
sophisticated international
and authentic local cuisine.

recreation
Swimming pool, tennis courts,
fitness centre, windsurfing,
sailing and watersports.
18-hole golf course nearby.

additional
24-hour room service and
concierge. Meeting facilities.
Dry cleaning service.
Secretarial service.
Boutiques. Beauty salon.
Cooking school.
Full service spa. Saunas.
Balinese massage.
Jacuzzis. Library.
Children's activities. Beach.

Close to the island's shopping and nightlife, yet removed just enough to ensure seclusion and tranquillity, The Legian is a dream destination for anyone seeking the best of all worlds in Bali.

Flanked by a quiet beach and lush rice paddies, sixty seven suites are set amidst landscaped tropical gardens. Inside, rich woods and elegant terazzo are used in a harmonious combination of contemporary and traditional design. Whatever the level of accommodation, you can count on spacious living areas, bathrooms and a private balcony or terrace. A selection of soon-to-be-opened villas will feature 40-foot private plunge pools and butler service.

At this resort, much of the activity takes place around the inviting two-tiered swimming pool. On its generous deck with plenty of places to enjoy the sun, the only thing between you and the Indian Ocean will be the beautiful Seminyak Beach.

The Restaurant opens onto the pool terrace and serves a wide range of Oriental and Western cuisine, while two traditional Balinese pavilions house The Pool Bar, perfect for an al fresco lunch or cocktails.

After a morning's shopping in nearby Kuta, come back and unwind in the Legian's spa. Here, an expertly-trained staff will pamper you with a variety of traditional and exotic Indonesian treatments ranging from facials to aromatherapy massage.

facts
Jalan Laksmana Seminyak, Kuta
T 62 361 730 622
F 62 361 730 623
67 suites.
Singles/Doubles:
From US$ 275 to 1,000
Plan: EP
Tax: 11% Service: 10%
Airport: 30 minutes.

dining
The restaurant offers the best
Asian specialities.
The Pool Bar: for breakfast, al-fresco
lunch, drinks and afternoon tea.

The Lobby Lounge & Bar:
for cocktails, afternoon tea and cigars.

recreation
Two-tiered swimming pool
and fitness centre.
18-hole golf course, tennis courts
and badminton nearby.

additional
24-hour room service. Meeting facilities
Traditional Asian spa. Sauna. Massage
Cable TV. Laundry service.
Airport transfer. Complimentary
shuttle service to shopping area.
Hi-Fi System in each suite.

amankila

facts
Manggis
T 62 363 41333
F 62 363 41555
35 suites.
Singles/Doubles:
From US$ 550 to 1700
Tax: 11%. Service charge: 10%
Plan: EP
Airport: 105 minutes

dining
The Terrace:
Western and Asian cuisine.
The Restaurant: sophisticated
Western and Indonesian cuisine.

The Beach Club: for lunch next
to the pool.

recreation
Swimming pools, water sports,
sailing, trekking and windsurfing.
Tennis courts nearby.

additional
24-hour room service.
Boutiques.
Library.
Beauty treatments.

Amankila means 'the peaceful hill'.

Well away from Bali's overcrowded tourist sites to the east of the island, this hotel's architect has succeeded in creating a tour de force that marries the hotel with its natural surroundings. The inspiration was the floating lake of Ujung, a former Balinese kingdom, and his design gives the impression that the 34 bungalows — some with private terrace — have existed forever, though in fact Amankila opened in 1992.

The rooms are remarkable: decorated with exquisite hand-carved furniture and sculptures of Hindu gods on the porches, they ensure privacy and seclusion. Perhaps the hotel's strongest point is the quality of the cuisine prepared with great care by a very talented chef. Amankila's main restaurant is a true marvel and justifiably considered to be among the best in the world. The triple-tiered swimming pools (inspired by the island's rice fields) merge and flow into one another and seem to plunge straight into the sea, thanks to a skilful optical illusion. The consequent vista across the Badung straits is quite staggering.

The magic formula of this hotel is simple, but is rarely found to be so well-applied: unbelievable service plus exceptional surroundings plus sophisticated cuisine equal a fabulous hotel.

You are not dreaming: this guide, which is not exactly dedicated to camping holidays, suggests you try camping in the middle of nowhere. But this is camping with a difference: twenty extremely luxurious, air-conditioned tents (with telephones only on request), all constructed and equipped with the greatest attention to detail.

Amanwana is truly the place for nature-lovers who want to see the exotic wildlife of the island. With monkeys and tortoises amongst its seemingly endless variety of species, it has been one of the most beautiful nature reserves for decades. On the other side of the island, you will have the opportunity to swim below the most stunning waterfalls.

Savour a selection of Indonesian and western specialities in the open-air pavilion facing the sea. Or one of the chefs will even prepare a private barbecue in front of your tent, if you wish.

For anyone still in any doubt about Amanwana, bear in mind that the Princess of Wales was a great fan — hard though it may have been to imagine her as a camper!

facts
T 62 371 22 233
F 62 371 22 288
20 Tents.
Tents: From US$ 615 to 750
Tax: 11%. Service charge: 10%
Plan: EP
Airport: 120 minutes by yacht

dining
The Dining Room: Indonesian
and international cuisine
in unique surroundings.

recreation
Windsurfing, scuba-diving,
fishing and trekking.

additional
Boutiques. Beauty salon. Library.
Massage.

amanusa

acts
PO Box 33, Nusa Dua
62 361 772 333
62 361 772 335
35 suites.
Singles/Doubles:
from US$ 550 to 950
Tax: 11%. Service charge: 10%
Plan: EP
Airport: 20 minutes

dining
The Terrace: Indonesian
and Thai cuisine.
The Restaurant: Italian cuisine.

recreation
Swimming pool, 18-hole golf course
and tennis courts.
Water sports nearby.

additional
24-hour room service. Beauty salon.
Banqueting and conferences facilities.
Cooking classes. Boutiques.
Massage. Excursions.
Library. Art gallery.

Exotic yet practical (only 20 minutes away from Denpasar airport), the very private and highly-regarded Amanusa — 'peaceful isle' in Sanskrit — represents a new level of accommodation in Bali.

This is a most relaxing resort; situated on the island's southern peninsula, the complex borders the Indian Ocean as well as adjoining the Bali Golf and Country Club. Its hilltop location offers views of the volcanic Mount Agung, surrounding mountains and the island of Nusa Penida.

Dispersed among luxuriant gardens and linked by footpaths to the main pavilion are the thatched-roof villas. There are only thirty-five, but together they create an atmosphere of calm, serenity and intimacy. Each one offers a large living area, a generously-sized bed and an enormous bathroom boasting a marble-tiled tub and a garden. There are also balconies to enjoy the best possible views of the ocean.

Ask for one of the eight suites with swimming pools, or on a larger scale, the Amanusa suite to experience the epitome of Indonesian comfort.

To witness the most extraordinary sunsets, plan a visit to the ancient Luhur Uluwatu temple, a sacred place with spectacular views.

nusalembonganresort

Between Bali and Nusa Penida, Nusa Lembongan is one of the last unspoilt islands in Indonesia's Badung Strait. Heavy on tradition and light on crowds and traffic, it is a pristine paradise that some say resembles the Bali of thirty years ago.

It is also home to the Nusa Lembongan Resort, an ultra-secluded retreat overlooking the sapphire blue waters of Sanghiang Bay. (The only way to get there is by a complimentary 45-minute catamaran ride from Bali's Benoa Harbour.)

Only twelve guest villas are offered, seven facing the ocean and five set in lush gardens. In each, traditional architecture and natural materials combine to create an authentic and relaxing environment. Besides a large canopied bed and sunken stone bathtub, there are also private terraces from which to enjoy the idyllic surroundings.

An open pavilion overlooking the beach offers a wide selection of delicious Indonesian and international cuisine. Personalised menus can also be created for intimate dining on several wooden decks overlooking the bay or outside your own villa.

Nusa Lembongan's surrounding reef is a protected marine park, offering a special attraction for divers. Surfers will appreciate some fine waves, and there is plenty of exploring to be done, whether it's in the island's mangroves, ancient underground dwellings or even the bat caves on a nearby island.

facts
P.O. Box 3846
T 62 361 725864
F 62 361 725866
Singles/Doubles:
From US$ 200 to 500
Tax: 21%
Plan: EP
Airport: 60 minutes

dining
The restaurant offers a wide selection of Indonesian and international cuisine.

Lounge bar for cocktails or after-dinner drinks.
Personalized menus are available for intimate dining.

recreation
Swimming pool.

additional
No television. Conference facilities. Library. Art Gallery.
Spa facilities. Gift shop.
Laundry/garment pressing.
Bali to Lembongan boat transfers.

HAPPY FEW

The Magazine of Excellence by
Guy Couloubrier since 1982

Tél. 33 1 43 80 31 25
Fax. 33 1 42 67 28 57

E mail : info@happyfewmag.com
Internet : www.happyfewmag.com

40, avenue Niel - 75017 PARIS

Fourseasonssayan

Where's the hotel?

That's the first question that comes to mind upon arriving at the Four Seasons at Sayan, sister property of the resort in Jimbaran Bay. This exotic retreat of eighteen suites and thirty-six villas is reached by crossing a suspension bridge that leads to the roof of a three story structure. Just past the lotus pond (yes, it's on the roof), a polished wood staircase descends to the reception area, an arresting stone space with a panoramic view on the Ayung River valley.

Surrounded by terraced rice fields and rolling hillsides, the resort's Frank Lloyd Wright-influenced design is both a contrast and compliment to its environment. Suites are contained within the main building and are decorated with rich teak and stone, custom made furnishings, locally-woven textiles and Balinese carvings.

Some villas are situated on the crest of the hill while others scatter down a verdant hillside leading to the river. All of them ensure total privacy and feature spacious teak decks with borderless plunge pools and private outdoor showers. Golf carts provide transportation between the main building, villas, river's edge swimming pool and Indonesian spa.

Last but certainly not least, a word for the cuisine. The chef prepares Balinese specialities and other Pan-Asian creations that are sure to please even the most demanding gourmet.

facts
Sayan - Ubud
T 62 361 977 577
F 62 361 977 588
18 suites and 36 villas.
Suites: From US$ 425
Villas: From US$ 575
Tax: 11%. Service charge: 10%
Plan: EP
Airport: 60 minutes

dining
Ayung Terrace: for international and regional dishes.
Riverside Café:
for casual poolside dining.
Jati Bar: for relaxing cocktails and after dinner drinks.

recreation
Outdoor swimming pool and Health & fitness centre.
18-hole golf courses 60 minutes from the resort.

additional
24-hour room service.
24-hour concierge. Gift Shop.
Laundry/dry cleaning.
Video CD player available.
Non-smoking rooms.
On-site car rental. Valet parking.
Sauna. Business services.
Steam Baths. Massage. Jacuzzi.
Traditional Indonesian herbal beauty and massage treatments.

On the marvellous island of Bali, Ubud is the cultural capital.

A day spent wandering its bustling little streets, browsing for trinkets and local arts and crafts, is enough to turn any traveller into a shopping fan. A stone's throw from the action, Pita Maha is a haven of peace.

Designed by a member of Ubud's royal family, the resort is modelled after a Balinese village — with an imperial touch here and there. An example is the lovely open-air Lobby Lounge, where you will be met with the customary welcome cocktail, the Brem Barong, within moments of your first arrival. Graced with intricate carvings that seem transplanted from one of the many temples nearby, it is the ideal spot to watch the sun melt into the Oos River and verdant rice paddies below.

Villas are well appointed with marble floors, wicker furniture, curving sunken bathtubs and glass panels that push aside to reveal private terraces. For the ultimate in indulgence, reserve one of the ten with its own refreshing plunge pool.

Another vantage point from which to enjoy the dreamlike view is the split-level restaurant. Set in an al fresco pavilion, it offers both Western and Oriental specialities and an impressive cellar.

A separate thatched building houses the spa, where it is highly recommended that you treat yourself to a traditional Balinese massage.

facts
Jalan Sanggingan, Ubud
T 62 361 974 330
F 62 361 974 329
24 villas.
Singles/Doubles: From US$ 300
Tax: 10% Service charge: 11%
Plan: EP
Airport: 45 minutes

dining
The al fresco restaurant serves western and oriental specialities.

recreation
Outdoor swimming pool.
18-Hole golf course nearby.

additional
24-hour villa service.
Laundry and dry-cleaning.
Boutiques.
Baby-sitting.
Excursions.

amandari

Amandari, 'the place where the spirits rest in peace, is a promising spot for anyone interested in Bali's indigenous arts and crafts, thanks mainly to the nearby village of Kedewatan. Its works make up the largest part of the hotel's impressive collection. The hotel's architect was inspired by the neighbouring villages, so the rooms are a subtle elaboration on the theme, constructed in teak and other woods from the workshops of local artisans. Even the least expensive room is a work of art in its own right.

And the service? Perhaps service is the wrong word — hospitality is closer to the mark.

In view of its location, Amandari is best suited to anyone interested in knowing more about the cultural aspects of the island (the temple of Pura Pusering Jagat near Pejeng is a must), rather than those who would prefer to lie on the beach (the nearest is an hour and a half away by car). However, the completely new spa will quickly make you forget how far you are from the sea by pampering your body with local herb and plants.

For a trip to paradise, look no further than the remarkable masseur, Mr. Ketut — anyone would happily kidnap him!

A superb place to stay for a few days.

facts
Ubud
T 62 361 975 333
F 62 361 975 335
30 suites.
Singles/Doubles:
From US$ 525 to 2300
Tax: 11%. Service charge: 10%
Plan: EP
Airport: 45 minutes

dining
The hotel's restaurant offers
the highest quality cuisine.

recreation
Swimming pool, health and fitness
centre, tennis court, rafting,
trekking and mountain biking.

additional
24-hour room service.
Library. Art gallery.
Massage.
Excursions. Gift shop.

amanjiwo

facts
Borobudur
T 62 293 788 333
F 62 293 788 355
36 suites.
Singles/Doubles:
From US$ 575 to 2200
Taxes: 11%. Service: 10%
Plan: EP
Airport: 60 minutes

dining
The Dining Room: Indonesian
and Western specialities.
Bar.

recreation
Swimming pool, two tennis courts.
18-hole golf course
and riding nearby.

additional
Boutiques.
Library. Art Gallery.
Massage. Meditation courses.
Excursions.

Right in the centre of Java, amidst terraced rice plantations and the Kedu Plain, Amanjiwo, or 'peaceful soul', rises up at the foot of Mount Menorah.

Opened just a few years ago, this hotel is one of the latest creations of Adrian Zecha and is a true ambassador of style and good taste. Uniquely set in a natural amphitheatre, it is modelled on Borobudur, the largest Buddhist monument in the world, which dates from the ninth century.

Amanjiwo is built mostly in a circular shape, which allows guests to enjoy the wonderful views of the surrounding countryside from both sides of their rooms. The suites (try for numbers 24 or 25) are decorated in restrained style, but are incomparably luxurious with marble floors, walls of rare woods, fitted stereo systems and a wonderful feeling of space.

All is absolutely faultless. The most beautiful suite has its own private swimming pool. Still not impressed? Bear in mind that it's more than sixty feet long!

The service is as one would expect — marvellous — and the staff are very friendly. On that subject, a word about the masseuses: after two hours in their capable hands, even the most jaded of travellers is guaranteed to reach seventh heaven.

gorakadan

Japan is famous for its ryokans, traditional inns that offer an opportunity to experience the true customs and atmosphere of a fascinating culture. Among ryokans, Gora Kadan is famous for being one of the best.

'Gora' refers to the hotel's location, a small town in the Hakone national park 100 miles south west of Tokyo. Best known for its natural hot spring baths, it is also the site of the former summer villa of the Kan-In-No-Mlya royal family, around which the hotel is built.

Not only your cares but your *clothes* will slip away not long after you enter this serene and lovely place. In order to enjoy total relaxation, guests are encouraged to wear kimonos as they pad around the premises, which include a covered swimming pool, Jacuzzi and spa offering Shiatzu and different massages.

All of the rooms are furnished in authentic Japanese style with Tatami mats, Shoji screens (and, lest you worry things will be too Zen-like, televisions). Bathrooms feature either a deep cypress wood tub or open-air bath. The suites open on balconies overlooking the mountains or, on the ground floor, private, meditative gardens. The exquisite service and amenities of Gora Kadan cannot be faulted. Furthermore, its perfectionism continues into the kitchen. One of the country's most reputable chefs orchestrates the multi-course Kaiseki-style meals that are included as part of your stay. Served in the manner of a Japanese tea ceremony, each dish is a work of art in itself, making dinner an almost theatrical experience not to be missed.

facts
Hakone-Machi,
Ashigara-Shimogun
T 81 460 2 3331
F 81 460 2 3334
28 rooms and 10 suites.
Singles/Doubles:
From JPY 100 000 to 120 000
Suites: From JPY 140 000
Tax: 5%
Plan: CP
Airport: 150 Km

dining
The restaurant offers
sophisticated local cuisine.

recreation
Indoor swimming pool.
18-hole golf course nearby.

additional
Limousine service on request.
Private steam sauna.
Jacuzzi. Spa.

carcosaserinegara

Carcosa Seri Negara is excellence itself. That one word really says it all, but let's expand on that: just five minutes from the town centre is an island of peace and luxury from another age. Set in the middle of sumptuous gardens stretching for many acres, Carcosa and Seri Negara are two colonial style mansions built at the turn of the century for the governor of the Malay states as well as honoured guests. After the visit of Queen Elizabeth II in 1989, the two mansions were opened so that the privileged of the whole world could enjoy the hotel's delights.

To start with Carcosa: this whitewashed colonial residence, completely restored in 1998, glistens in the sun above the lake and the gardens. Surrounded by small verandas, the main staircase leads towards the suites, all of which are incomparable. Seri Negara is only a few minutes away: with majestic doorways, terraces and abundant gardens, the decor is roughly similar to its sister mansion.

In this instance, the staircase leads towards six ravishing suites, in shades of rose or salmon and furnished in great taste thanks to Malay works of art and Regency style furniture (opt for Seri Kinabalu suite with its two verandas or Seri Makmur) If you are dining in town, do not miss 'Mango Tree', an excellent restaurant.

facts
Taman Tasik Perdana
T 60 3 2282 1888
F 60 3 2282 7888
13 suites.
Suites: From MYR 950 to 3500
Tax and service charge included.
Plan: EP
Airport: 50 minutes

dining
Mashuri: contemporary modern cuisine.
Seri Negara Drawing Room &
Verandah: for light meals.
Titiwangsa: for cocktails.

recreation
Swimming pool, tennis court,
fitness centre, jogging track.
18-hole golf course nearby
(clubs and shoes are provided by
the hotel)

additional
Meeting and conference facilities.
24-hour room service.
Business centre.
Sauna. Massage.

acts
alan Teluk Datai
60 4 959 1088
60 4 959 1168
81 rooms and 7 suites.
ingles/Doubles:
om MYR 1400 to 1550
uites: From MYR 2500 to 6000
ax and service charge included.
an: EP
irport: 30 minutes

ining
le restaurant serves Mediterranean
uisine, international and local
pecialties.

The Gulai House: Malay & indian food.
Kamogawa: Japanese cuisine.
The Pool Bar: for quick lunches
next to the pool.
New Beach Bar.

recreation
Swimming pool, fitness centre, billiards,
snorkelling and water sports.
18-hole golf course and tennis nearby.

additional
Conference and meeting facilities,
24-hour room service and concierge.
Library. Massage. Boutiques. Hair salon.
New 'Jamu nature' Spa.

Designed to radiate a luxuriant but natural feel, the Andaman is one of two completely new resorts of great comfort situated nearby its illustrious predecessor, the Datai.

Its difference from the Datai is perhaps the ambience. This hotel is a little more lively and preterred by families with children.

All the rooms are decorated in authentic Malay style using light woods and natural-coloured fabrics and are lavishly equipped with air-conditioning and satellite television. If possible, try to reserve one of the rooms with a sea view. And if your pocket allows it, pick the Malay, the Japanese or the presidential suite — they are definitely among the best.

There are varied sporting activities: the course at the Datai Bay Golf Club is a masterpiece, tennis courts are a few minutes away by car and every kind of non-motorised water sport is available.

Finally, do take a walk in the 50-million-year-old rainforest and admire the flora and fauna of an area, which is still unspoiled. Let's hope it stays that way.

thedatai

Open less than a decade, The Datai already enjoys a high reputation in south east Asia.

Built in the midst of virgin forest, the hotel rises like a teak cathedral with its architecture blending Japanese and stylised pagoda roofs. The Datai is not the place for those who want lively evenings. There is no cabaret, no piano bar and not one nightclub for miles around. Here, it is the outdoor and not the indoor types who set the scene: trekking, mountain-cycling and deep-sea fishing are among the main activities.

The villas have air-conditioning and humidity controls and give on to verandas and terraces. All are exquisite and their balconies have superb views of the jungle or the Andaman Sea.

The only noise comes from the surrounding animals: monkeys swinging from tree to tree and birds which you can admire with the help of Irshad Mobarak, the resident expert on all aspects of the hotel.

A small drawback: there are 500 steps to the beach. However, if you're not so energetic, the hotel provides golf carts to transport you.

Try to visit between November and March when the weather is at its best.

facts
Jalan Teluk Datai
T 60 4 959 2500
F 60 4 959 2600
94 rooms and 14 suites.
Singles/Doubles:
From MYR 1260 to 5600
Tax and service charge included.
Plan: EP
Airport: 30 minutes

dining
The Pavilion: Thai cuisine.
The Beach Club: for lunch
and dinner.

The Dining Room: Western
and Malay cuisine.

recreation
Two swimming pools,
two tennis courts,
fitness centre, windsurfing,
scuba-diving and sailing.
18-hole golf course nearby.

additional
Meeting rooms. Satellite TV.
Car rental. Boutiques.
Spa. Beauty Salon.
Sauna. Massage.

tanjongjararesort

facts
Batu 8 Off Dungun
T 60 9 845 11 00
F 60 9 845 12 00
100 rooms and suites.
Singles/Doubles:
From MYR 700 to 2070
Tax and service charge included.
Plan: EP
Airport: 70 Km

dining
Di Atlas Sungei: for Malaysian
and international specialities.
The Nelayan: for seafood specialities.
The Teratai Terrace: for light meals.

recreation
Two swimming pools,
two tennis courts, fitness centre,
kayaking, fishing, windsurfing,
water-skiing and scuba diving.
18-hole golf courses nearby.

additional
Room service. Meeting facilities.
Concierge. Laundry service.
Foreign currency exchange.
Baby-sitting services upon request.
Limousine service.
Massage.Gift shop.

On a forty-two acre beachfront on Malaysia's eastern seaboard, Tanjong Jara feels like a refuge at the ends of the earth. Opened in 1979, the resort was awarded one of the world's most prestigious architecture prizes its design inspired by 'Istanas', elegant, wooden palaces that housed the Malay sultans of long ago. Recently its beauty was enhanced (and facilities made state-of-the-art) by a renovation that has incorporated styles from all around the Malaysian archipelago.

Housed in bungalows along the coastline, the guest accommodations recreate seventeenth-century indigenous dwellings and are furnished to perfection with rich textiles and natural materials. Most luxurious of all are the individual beach cottages, with tropical gardens, outdoor sunken tubs and covered terraces leading onto the gardens and beach — the perfect place to watch the sun set over the South China Sea.

In addition to water sports including kayaking, sailing and diving, there are opportunities to the explore the environmental side of the peninsula as well.

Authentic Malaysian cuisine can be enjoyed in 'Di Atlas Sungei', affording both river and sea views, or in 'The Nelayan' on the shore, where seafood is the order of the day.

The panorama as you approach Soneva Fushi by air is breathtaking: sand-framed atolls sprinkled over a turquoise sea, surrounded by emerald lagoons and brilliant coral reefs. The resort itself is no less impressive.

Set on the privately-owned and formerly uninhabited island of Kunfunadhoo, the idea behind this hotel (the first in its part of the Maldives) was to offer a Robinson Crusoe-style existence enhanced with the amenities of modern day life. While we can't speak for Mr. Robinson, today's castaways will certainly be pleased with the result.

A handful of secluded, thatched-bamboo villas are set on the waterfront and discreetly integrated into the lush landscape. Outfitted with the natural woods and textiles of Asia, all have private sitting areas and bathrooms opening on to a enclosed, tropical garden. As for those anything-but-primitive amenities, they include sound systems with extra speakers in the bathrooms (of course!) and television and video players on request.

From simple barbecues to gourmet feasts blending a world of cuisines, dining options are many. Add to this a comprehensive spa and full menu of water sports — including an on-site diving school — and Soneva Fushi is sure to fulfil even your most escapist dreams.

facts
Kunfunadhoo Island
T 960 230 304
F 960 230 374
65 rooms and suites.
Singles/Doubles:
From US$ 250 to 535
Villas: From US$ 410 to 1450
Plan: EP
Tax included.
Airport: 25 minutes

dining
The main restaurant for breakfast and dinner.

Me Dhuniye: for a blend of Eastern and Western food - breakfast and dinner.
Mihiree Mitha: for buffet lunch.

recreation
Fitness centre, diving, snorkelling, jogging trail, cycling, badminton, fishing and all water sports.

additional
24-hour room service. Laundry and valet service. Babysitting. Excursions. Spa with holistic beauty & body treatments.

facts
Lankanfushi Island
T 960 33 66 63
F 960 33 66 64
44 suites and residences.
Suites: From US$ 500
Tax included.
Service charge: 10%
Plan: EP
Airport: 15 minutes

dining
The restaurant serves
international cuisine.
Over water bar with dining areas.
In-villa dining.

recreation
Swimming pool, deep-sea fishing,
snorkelling, waterskiing, canoeing,
tennis courts and diving school.

additional
Library & internet access.
Excursions. Six Senses Spa.
Video and CD library.
Laundry & Valet Service.
Gift Shop. Baby Sitting.
Air-conditioned and over head fan.

Room with a sea view not quite what you're looking for? Water's-edge bungalow doesn't cut it either? Soneva Gili may be exactly the right place for you.

Forty-four bi-level suites and residences are decked out in sustainable woods, natural materials and traditional fabrics, enhanced by modern amenities. All have bathtubs with sea views, marvellous private floating platforms to lounge upon and some have top-level Jacuzzis. For the ultimate in privacy, book one of the six stand-alone residences in the middle of the lagoon — accessible by boat only.

The restaurant and Lagoon Bar offer one of the finest culinary experiences in the islands, featuring just-harvested produce and international wines. Dinners can also be served under the stars on your floating platform (we defy you to find a more romantic experience than that!)

A full range of watersports is available, windsurfing, water-skiing and wake boarding being just a few. Soneva Gili also features its own state-of-the-art diving school, where professional instructors can train beginners to be PADI certified in less than a week, or escort more advanced divers to spectacular locations nearby.

Fourseasonsmaldives

According to the brochure, the Four Seasons at Kuda Huraa is a place that approaches paradise on earth. If that sounds like an exaggeration, we encourage you to see for yourself.

On this completely private island in the Maldives, there's just you, the hotel and... the fish. So if you come, it is an advantage to been keen on water sports and sunsets or really in love.

The resort consists of thatched-roof bungalows and villas brimming over with understated luxury and well-considered creature comforts. Among them, don't hesitate to book the water bungalows; on stilts over the lagoon, they are truly superb, totally private and offer 360–degree views of the ocean, thanks to transparent bedroom walls facing the water.

Diving instructor Raymond Howe maintains that whatever your level of aptitude, the diving here is the finest anywhere. If you're not so adventurous, the swimming pool is so beautiful and originally designed you can take a dip or simply persuade yourself you are admiring a work of art.

East-meets-west cuisine awaits in the beautiful surroundings of the Baraabaru restaurant, while the Nautilus. And for those lucky really-in-love types, romantic dinners can be set up in the privacy of your bungalow.

facts
North Male Atoll
T 960 444 888
F 960 441 188
106 bungalows and villas.
Singles/Doubles:
From US$ 350 to 2280
Service charge: 10%
Plan: CP
Airport: 20 Km

dining
Cafe Huraa: continental dining.
Baraabaru Speciality restaurant:
Maldivian and Indian cuisine.

Poolside Terrace & Bar:
light snacks & refreshments.
Nautilus Lounge: cocktails
and refreshments with music.
Reef Club: Mediterranean cuisine.

recreation
Swimming pool, diving centre,
water sports and gymnasium.

additional
Air-conditioning. Clinic. Laundry.
Foreign currency exchange.
Satellite TV. Spa. Massage.
Excursions. Library.

facts
P.O. Box 456, Pasay City
T 63 2 759 4040
F 63 2 759 4044
29 casitas.
Singles/Doubles:
From US$ 475 to 2100
Tax: 10%. Service charge: 10%
Plan: EP
Airport: 60 minutes

dining
The Restaurant: Continental
and Filipino cuisine.
The Beach Club: for light meals.
Lobby Bar: for cocktails.

recreation
Tennis courts, windsurfing,
scuba-diving, sailing, fishing,
jogging, swimming and biking.

additional
Meeting facilities.
24-hour room service.
Boutiques. Babysitting. Library.
Art gallery. Massage.
DVD, Laserdiscs and video tape
recorders available on request.

Opened in 1993 by the founder of the world-wide Aman group of properties is a place for those who want to leave the city as far behind as possible and take refuge in nature, without of course, losing a shred of comfort.

Amanpulo ('the peaceful isle') is a private atoll where you arrive by plane from Manila.

You will find yourself in a small house of six hundred square feet in Philippine style (choose either villa number 39 or villa number 40 — they have the best views) where you will be in total harmony with nature.

You will be offered little buggies to use to make a tour of the island (prepare yourself for beaches of white sand and unsurpassed beauty) and, besides the usual features of each room, you will find compact disc players, satellite phones and television.

If you do not want to see anyone, then that is simply not a problem: the secluded terrace of each casita (on the beach or on the hill) guarantees your privacy.

A holiday destination of the highest calibre.

thegalleryevason

The Gallery Evason has been the talk of Singapore since its recent opening in the city's trendy Robertson Quay district.

Rising above a complex that includes restaurants, speciality boutiques and a dance club, its Bauhaus-by-day, neon-by-night façade serves as a daring landmark next to the Singapore River.

Celebrated in architecture and design journals, the hotel's public spaces are the epitome of urban chic. Industrial elements such as stainless steel give them a definite edge, while brightly-coloured cushions and indoor foliage keep things from feeling too stark.

Frosted glass, timber panelling and sleek metallic details lend a calm, luminous feel to the guest rooms, whose double-glazed windows reveal cityscapes and views of the river. The very latest in technological amenities are what put them over the top. Step out of bed in the dark and motion sensors activate a lighted path to your bathroom.

Another basic element — water — is put to good use, whether in the 'liquid curtains' of the comprehensive spa or the cantilevered glass-sided lap pool.

While it goes without saying that the Gallery Evason is an excellent choice for business travellers, certain among them have an especially attractive option. The hotel's entire fifth floor — with an all-female staff — is reserved for women travelling alone.

facts
76 Robertson Quay
T 65 235 3120
F 65 235 3590
223 rooms and suites.
Singles/Doubles:
From SG$ 245 to 470
Tax and service charge not included.
Plan: EP

dining
The restaurant serves Asian
fusion cuisine.
The Bar and The Pool Bar for drinks.

recreation
Glass-sided rooftop pool.
18-hole golf course and tennis
courts nearby.

additional
Function and meeting rooms.
In-room check-in. Unlimited internet
access. GSM cellular phone on
request. Cable TV. Health spa.

raffleshotel

facts
One Beach Road
T 65 337 1886
F 65 339 7650
103 suites.
Suites: From S$ 650 to 6000
Tax: 4%. Service charge: 10%
Plan: EP
Airport: 20 minutes

dining
Tiffin Room and Raffles Grill:
international curry buffet
and continental fine dining.
Five restaurants for a choice of
quick or sophisticated meals.

Bar & Billard Room, Long Bar and
Writer's Bar: for cocktails.

recreation
24-hour swimming pool
and fitness centre.

additional
24-hour room service, concierge
and business centre.
Limousine airport transfer.
Dry-cleaning service. Boutiques.
Beauty salon.
Sauna. Jacuzzi.

A flawless diamond, a little marvel, the grande dame of Singapore, an heirloom from the days of British rule — all this and more can be said of Raffles.

Established in 1887 and named after the city's founder, Sir Thomas Stamford Raffles, the hotel quickly rose to become *the* fashionable tourist destination between 1880 and 1939. In 1989, the hotel underwent a major renovation to restore it to its former pre-Great War glory.

The suites have six-metre high ceilings, floors of dark, impeccable hardwood, imposing fans set above enormous beds and precious works of art. On the balconies, rattan chairs and small tables look out over the lush gardens and courtyards where the languid and humid breeze drifts over you.

The service is faultless: a butler will see to your every need — wake you with tea and newspaper, book a restaurant table or a plane ticket. In short, the smallest effort on your part is impossible.

If you cannot finance actually staying here, at least take tea in the Tiffin Room. At 3.30 p.m. precisely, the waiters stand in line to welcome you, and proceed to serve the perfect afternoon tea.

theoriental

For more than a century, the Oriental in Bangkok has welcomed the great and the good of the world.

On the banks of the Chao Phraya River, surrounded by lush gardens and terraces, the hotel is less than ten minutes away from the commercial district and the main shops of the city. At its heart is the old wing, famous for legendary litterary guests such as Somerset Maugham, Graham Greene and James Michener. Even contemporary authors are fans (John le Carre finished 'The Honourable Schoolboy' while staying here). Throughout the building you will find guestrooms furnished in teak, mahogany and traditional Thai silks.

With a staff of one thousand for four hundred rooms, you will definitely feel well-cared for. At the front desk, your key is handed to you without your having to give your name or room number — truly professional service.

The Oriental has nine restaurants, including probably the best French one in the region. There is also a world-class spa across the river, reached by boat (a former American president had a massage there every day of his stay).

Without a doubt, the Oriental is still one of the greatest hotels in the world.

In Bangkok, the restaurant of the moment is 'Reflexions' with its ultra smart and sophisticated design.

facts
48 Oriental Avenue
T 66 2 659 9000
F 66 2 236 1937
362 rooms and 34 suites.
Singles/Doubles: From US$ 250
Suites: From US$ 420 to 2000
Tax: 7.7%. Service charge: 10%
Plan: EP
Airport: 25 minutes

dining
Sala Rim Naam:
Traditional Thai cuisine.
Le Normandie: French cuisine.
The China House: Chinese cuisine.

Lord Jim's: for seafood.
Ciao: Italian cuisine.
The Verandah: for light meals.
Riverside Terrace: for out-door dining.

recreation
Two outdoor swimming pools,
tennis court, squash court
and fitness centre.

additional
Meeting and banqueting rooms.
Concierge. 24-hour room service.
Business centre. Boutiques.
Spa. Sauna. Thai cooking school.

facts
Mae Rim-Samoeng Old Road
T 66 53 298 181
F 66 53 298 190
75 suites.
Singles/Doubles: From US$ 320
Tax: 18.5%
Plan: EP
Airport: 30 minutes

dining
Sala Mae Rim: for the highest quality northern Thai cuisine.
Poolside Bar: for lunch and dinner by the pool.

recreation
Swimming pool, two tennis courts and a fitness centre.
Four world-class 18-hole golf courses nearby.

additional
Conference and banqueting rooms.
24-hour concierge and room service.
Secretarial service.
Boutique. Spa. Massage.
Jacuzzis. Children's activities.

The only luxury-class establishment in northern Thailand, the Regent has become the standard for all hotels in the region since it opened in 1995.

Ideally situated in the foothills of the Mae Sa valley, the complex has been designed to reflect the architecture and 700 year-old culture of this part of the country. It is made up of a small group of pavilions, each containing several suites that look out over a mosaic of rice paddies and lakes.

Each suite measures more than 650 square feet and contains Thai paintings, works of art, polished teak floors and very large bathrooms. The level of comfort is of the highest order and the spacious terrace, from where you can take in the mountains all around, or have dinner, is a delight.

The omnipresent staff are thoughtful and considerate; it is easy to see why so many celebrities (Hilary Clinton, recently) have already sampled the charms of this little gem of the international hotel élite.

Avid shoppers will be pleased to learn that the town is a shopping heaven and that the hotel organises visits to the best shops for silk, silver, furniture and much more.

chivasomresort

Thailand's Chiva Som has been called the best health resort in the world. With a construction cost of $26 million, it should be! No expense was spared to turn this seven-acre site on the island of Hua Hin into a paradise for mind, body and spirit.

Your stay begins with a private consultation to design a programme appropriate to your needs. Whether that is combating stress, ageing or smoking, or simply to regain a sense of health and well-being, an astounding array of therapies is available. The ultra-modern spa features fifteen rooms for treatments and massages, French hydrotherapy baths, saunas and jacuzzis and a mineral-rich flotation chamber. The nearby Bathing Pavilion houses a huge indoor pool and hot and cold pools carpeted with pebbles to massage the feet. There is a second, beachfront swimming pool and a high-tech gym offering classes in everything from Thai boxing to Yoga.

The "mind" part is covered by stimulating lectures and demonstrations such as cooking classes. Speaking of which, Chiva Som's chef will make you a believer in the gourmet potential of healthy, organic food (yes, wine and champagne are allowed with dinner). Perhaps the most relaxing spot will be your room, one of 57 in traditional Thai pavilions surrounded by lotus ponds and waterfalls. Built of native wood and furnished with antiques and cultural artifacts, all promise serenity.

facts
73/4 Petchkasem Road
T 66 32 536 536
F 66 32 511 154
Singles/Doubles: from US$ 420 to 800
Suites: From US$ 640 to 1800
Plan: MAP
Airport: 140 km

dining
The restaurant serves a selection of western and Asian specialities.

recreation
Swimming pools, fitness centre
18-hole golf course, tennis courts and riding nearby.

additional
24-hour room service.
Meeting and banquet facilities.
Health centre & Spa.
Sauna. Massage.

amanpuri

facts
Pansea Beach
T 66 76 324 333
F 66 76 324 100
40 suites and 30 villas.
Singles/Doubles:
From US$ 500 to 1200
Tax: 11%. Service charge: 10%
Plan: EP
Airport: 20 minutes

dining
The Terrace: Excellent Thai
and European cuisine.
The Restaurant: Italian cuisine.
Bar for cocktails and quick meals.

recreation
Swimming pool, six tennis courts,
gymnasium, windsurfing,
scuba-diving, water-skiing.
18-hole golf course nearby.

additional
24-hour room service.
Foreign currency exchange.
Limousine service.
Beauty salon.
Library. Boutiques.
Sauna. Massage.

Adrian Zecha, the talented creator of Aman properties, has spent millions transforming a small cooonut plantation on the island of Phuket into an earthly paradise. Since 1988, Amanpuri has become an international yardstick at lightning speed, and has rapidly established its reputation on five continents.

Meaning 'Heaven of peace' in Sanskrit, Amanpuri is all simply magnificent. The rooms feature the same exquisite teak as in sister properties, the parquet floors are impeccably waxed, the beds and pillows of the highest quality.

Each individual pavilion — 103 and 105 are the best — has around 900 square feet and views of either the Andaman Sea or the orchid gardens.

All are decorated in restrained Zen style, with air-conditioning, stereo, very nice bathtubs and a *Sala* (small terrace) as well as beautiful Thai works of art. Aside from the shower fittings and mirrors (which come from Paris), everything, from A to Z, has been designed by Ed Tuttle.

The service is pure courtesy and consideration, thanks once again to the innate charm of the Thai people.

You will not be surprised, therefore, to hear that Richard Branson, the Aga Khan and many others put Amanpuri high on their lists.

thechedi

Surrounded by the brilliant blue Andaman Sea is the popular Thai island of Phuket. Nestled in peaceful seclusion on Phuket's most exclusive bay is The Chedi.

Taking inspiration from its natural environment, this resort is a tropical oasis where coconut palms sway above cottages cascading down to a white sand beach. Its design incorporates elements of local culture, such as historical pieces of native art that have been collected, restored and installed on the grounds.

All cottages were furnished with elegance and tranquillity in mind. Handcrafted teak floors, Thai textiles, 100% cotton Chiang Mai bed linens and specially-created toiletries are just a few of the luxuries in store for the discerning guest. Each has a private verandah with deck chairs overlooking the sea.

The Chedi's restaurants offer a range of imaginative menus fusing European, exotic eastern and Thai cuisine. There is the elegant Lom Talay for refined cuisine backed by classical Thai music, the outdoor Beach Restaurant for an impressive variety of freshly-caught seafood, and the Sunset Bar for cocktails and wonderful views.

Non-motorised sports are offered on Pansea Beach, while water skiing, diving and golf are easily arranged. The recently-built onsite spa offers no less than nine different therapeutic massages by some of the most experienced therapists in Thailand.

facts
Pansea Bay 118 Moo 3
Choeng Talay Talang
T 66 76 324 017
F 66 76 324 252
108 cottages.
Singles/Doubles:
from US$ 160 to 520
Tax:7%. Service charge:10%.
Plan: EP

dining
Lomtalay Restaurant:
for Thai and Asian cuisine.
The Beach Restaurant:
for barbecued seafood (during high season only).
Sunset Cafe and Bar serves a menu that fuses the cuisines of East and West.
Beach Bar: for light snacks and cocktails.

recreation
Swimming pool, tennis courts and watersports.
Several 18 hole golf courses nearby.

additional
Spa. Boutique. Gift shop.
Babysitting service.
Children's activities.
Laundry and dry cleaning.
Airport transfer. Car rental.
Internet service. Library.

anamandara

Ana Mandara means 'beautiful home for the guests'.

The phrase is lovely, but it only begins to describe the splendour and tranquillity of this unique resort on the edge of Nha Trang Bay. Comprised of sixteen villas surrounded by five acres of tropical foliage, it perfectly embodies the rich culture and unique flavours of Vietnam.

Natural wood and rattan furnishings are found throughout the sixty-eight rooms and suites, whose decor is modern with southeast Asian art and details. Simple, serene and bathed in golden light, each of them come with a covered terrace and all the latest amenities.

Adjacent to the pristine private beach is a stunning open-air restaurant serving gourmet east/west cuisine, while next to a bamboo garden is the lounge bar, for light meals and nightly performances of traditional music.

An extensive water sports centre offers snorkelling, diving, jet-ski and parasailing among many other activities, but for those seeking a more quiet form of recreation, arrangements can be made for boat trips to a picnic offshore.

Gracious service, refined and restful ambience, captivating scenery… suffice it to say that thanks to places like Ana Mandara, the world is rediscovering Vietnam as a unique and rewarding holiday destination.

facts
Beachside Tran Phu Boulevard
T 84 58 829 829
F 84 58 829 629
68 rooms
Singles/Doubles: From US$ 160
Tax: 5% Service charge: 10%
Plan: EP
Airport: 10 minutes

dining
The restaurant serves
international cuisine.

recreation
Swimming pool, health club,
fitness centre and all watersports.

additional
24-hour room service.
Meeting and banquet facilities.
Laundry and dry cleaning.
Babysitting.
Foreign currency exchange.
Boutiques.

unitedstates

Elizabeth Taylor honeymooned here (at least once). Gable and Lombard used Bungalow number 4 for clandestine trysts before his divorce. Howard Hughes lived here for nearly three decades, and Marilyn Monroe rented Room 305 for two years running. Of course, we're talking about the Beverly Hills Hotel.

Built in 1912 and currently owned by the Sultan of Brunei, the 'Pink Palace' was recently renovated at a cost of millions. Today the peach and apricot decor, enhanced by Art Nouveau ceilings, gilded balconies and massive Italian chandeliers, just oozes that starstruck elegance that made this hotel a legend.

Each of the rooms and suites is individually furnished, most with fireplaces or terraces (the best overlook the pool). Surrounded by palms and fragrant gardens, the famous bungalows offer the ultimate in privacy (and walls you wish could talk!).

Even today, meetings between producers and actors take place in the famous 'Polo Lounge'. A less expensive option is the tiny 'Fountain Coffee Shop', known for its milkshakes, pancakes and the occasional celebrities who order them.

Outside, at the end of a long day's wheeling and dealing — or not — finish up at L'Orangerie, which for the last 15 years has maintained the title of best French restaurant in town, or 'Chadwick', a new and very hip spot.

facts
9641 Sunset Boulevard, Ca
T 1 310 276 2251
F 1 310 281 2905
169 rooms and 36 suites.
Singles/Doubles:
From US$ 325 to 400
Suites: From US$ 625 to 3050
Tax: 15.2%
Plan: EP
Airport: 30 minutes

dining
The Polo and Cabana Club:
for lunch.

The Polo Lounge: for lunch, dinner and supper.
The Tea Lounge: for tea.

recreation
Outdoor swimming pool, two tennis courts and fitness centre.

additional
Meeting and banqueting facilities.
Concierge. 24-hour room service.
Dry-cleaning service. Boutiques.
Secretarial service.
Limousine service. Spa. Massage.
Jacuzzis. Video players and CD player in every room.

facts
300 South Doheny Drive, Ca
T 1 310 273 2222
F 1 310 859 3824
179 rooms and 106 suites.
Singles/Doubles:
From US$ 325 to 405
Tax and service charge included.
Plan: EP
Airport: 30 minutes

dining
Gardens Restaurant:
for international cuisine.
The Café: for all day meals.
Windows Lounge: for tea and cocktails.

recreation
Swimming pool and fitness centre.

additional
Conference and meeting facilities.
24-hour concierge, butler and room
service. Secretarial service.
Limousine service. Parking. Jacuzzis.
Video players.

As with all Four Seasons hotels around the world, the one in Los Angeles enjoys excellent qualities: a perfect location (just minutes from Rodeo Drive, the famed shopping street), an avalanche of marble in the lobby and a superb collection of art.
The guest rooms are decorated in soothing natural tones, enhanced by flower arrangements and comptuous bathrooms. Most of them have private balconies (a true luxury in this part of Los Angeles). The rooftop swimming pool has a slightly surreal look about it; surrounded by foliage and little cabanas, it seems to float in a world of its own high above the traffic and noise of the city.
'Gardens' restaurant (where breakfast is certainly the best in town) sets the standard against which the most influential members of the film industry measure all other establishments.
Hugh Grant, Kenneth Brannagh, Isabella Rossellini and many others never miss a chance to enjoy the relaxed but very chic atmosphere here whenever they are in the neighborhood.
Incidentally, animals are allowed, making it the only local hotel of this standard with such a policy. Advantage or disadvantage? For its minimalist ambience and surprising dishes, 'Tengu', one of the latest restaurants in Los Angeles is worth a visit.

Claudia and Marcus hang out at the Mondrian, a 1950's sixteen-storey building entirely redesigned by style guru of the moment, Frenchman Philippe Starck. Here's what they might say.

Claudia: Did you catch the mahogany doors at the entrance? They've gotta be 30-feet high. Pretty cool, huh? C'mon, let's hit the Sky Bar – I've heard it's where the A-list chills out. Wow! Check out that L.A view! Awesome!

Marcus: Isn't that Ralph Fiennes over there?

Claudia: Between George Clooney and Cameron Diaz? Could be! Enter Naomi and Darren.

Naomi: Some hotel, huh? I'm telling you, Stark's really it. It's so L.A! God, I love this place! Why don't we head to Coco Pazzo? I wanna do some serious networking with Al Pacino. Did I tell you I was in Coco Pazzo in New York? Oh, my God…. Oh, hi Leonardo, how're you doing?

Darren: Y'know that everything here has been designed by Starck? Even the rooms! You can tell it right away – it's so minimalist. It really speaks to me.

Marcus: You know what? You can buy the stuff! They've got a catalogue of the whole thing!

Naomi: Right! I'm gonna buy a vase and an ashtray. Not that I smoke of course! At least not since I took up yoga at Linda Guber's well-being centre. She's so great and she and I are so close…

facts
8440 Sunset Boulevard, Ca
T 1 213 650 8999
F 1 213 650 5215
245 rooms and suites.
Singles/Doubles:
From US$ 240 to 350
Suites: From US$ 375 to 2600
Plan: EP
Airport: 30 minutes

dining
Coco Pazzo serves contemporary and innovative cuisine.
Patio Garden Restaurant.
Sky Bar: for cocktails.

recreation
Heated swimming pool,
24-hour state-of-the-art gymnasium,
indoor and outdoor fitness.
18-hole golf course and tennis nearby.

additional
Steam rooms. Saunas. Jacuzzis.
Non-smoking rooms available.
Banqueting and meeting facilities.
24-hour room service and concierge.
Portable telephones and computers upon request. Business centre.
Children's play area.

facts

7500 Wilshire Boulevard, Ca
T 1 310 275 5200
F 1 310 274 2851
275 rooms and 120 suites.
Singles/Doubles:
From US$ 325 to 480
Suites: From US$ 465 to 7500
Tax: 15.2%
Plan: EP
Airport: 30 minutes

dining

The Dining Room:
for international cuisine.

The Lobby Lounge: for breakfast,
lunch and dinner.
The Bar: for evening cocktails.

recreation

Outdoor heated swimming pool
and state-of-the-art fitness centre.

additional

24-hour room service and concierge.
Multi-lingual staff. Business centre.
Meeting facilities. Private garage.
Beauty salon. Health Spa. Sauna.
Massage. Steam bath.

At the crossroads of the famous Rodeo Drive and facing the Hollywood Hills, the Regent Beverly Wilshire is extremely well-situated in the centre of Beverly Hills.

Behind the superb baroque-style facade, the impressive and imposing entrance hall sets the tone with a magnificent chandelier lighting up marble and mahogany. Inside this establishment built in 1926 and completely renovated in 1999, you will find a strong European influence (with superb Aubusson tapestries) as well as genial staff who will quickly take you in hand. Try to stay in the main part of the building rather than the wings because the rooms there are more sophisticated, both in terms of their decor and the finish of their Greek and Italian marble bathrooms.

Almost beyond description, on the eighth floor is the well-named Presidential suite: with its enormous entrance hall flanked with marble columns and its 4,000 square feet, you will not be short of space! The new Penthouse suites with their wrap-around balconies, and the Veranda suites on the top floor, are two equally fortunate choices. So too are the new themed suites designed by Gucci, Dior and Hermès. Finally, some recommended restaurants in Beverly Hills: 'Spago' and 'Citrus' have reputations as unparalleled as their prices and, on Melrose Avenue, 'Eclipse' is also very much in vogue.

aubergedusoleil

Originally, the Auberge du Soleil was a restaurant opened in 1981 by Claude Rouas. A few years later it grew into a hotel, which resembles a Mediterranean villa in the middle of acres of vineyards and olive groves. Before long, the hotel began to attract celebrities from the film and music industry and wealthy businessmen.

There are two parts to the resort. The main building houses large and romantic rooms, but the cottages in the gardens are what you should try to book.

In each suite (named after French provinces), you'll come across charming furniture from the southeastern of the United States as well as fireplaces, compact disc playesr, video players and terraces.

The spa services are marvellous; you fill in a form so that the staff know what kind of service to provide before starting you on a two-hour course in relaxation — but for a rather astronomical price!

Aside from touring local vineyards, there isn't a great deal to do in the area except taking in the extraordinary air and light. And then of course sampling the hotels sublime cuisine combining Asian and Californian styles, accompanied by the best wines from a remarkably well-stocked cellar.

facts
180 Rutherford Hill Road, Ca
T 1 707 963 1211
F 1 707 963 8764
50 rooms and suites.
Singles/Doubles:
From US$ 350 to 575
Suites: From US$ 750 to 2000
Tax and service charge not included.
Plan: EP
Airport: 120 Km

dining
The restaurant serves breakfast, lunch and dinner.

recreation
Swimming pool, tennis courts and fitness centre.
18-hole golf courses nearby.

additional
24-hour room service. Concierge. Valet service. Whirlpool. Sauna. Massage. Jacuzzi.
Art galleries and antique shops nearby.

theshermanhouse

facts
2160 Green Street, Ca
T 1 415 563 3600
F 1 415 563 1882
8 rooms and 6 suites.
Singles/Doubles:
From US$ 360 to 445
Suites: From US$ 675 to 750
Tax: 14%. Service charge included.
Plan: CP
Airport: 35 Km

dining
The kitchen offers a delicate combination of French and Californian cuisine.

recreation
18-hole golf course, tennis and water sports nearby.

additional
24-hour room service.

A grand Victorian-style house with views of the Golden Gate bridge and San Francisco Bay, the Sherman House is a small hotel in size, but one of the greatest when it comes to service and presentation.

In 1876, Leander Sherman, a passionate music-lover, wanted to create an exceptional hotel in order to provide the best conditions possible for the great names of the artistic world such as Caruso and Paderewski.

Over one hundred years later, it can be said that Mr. Sherman's achievement still flourishes in the stunning rooms and suites boasting Biedermeier and French Second Empire furniture. It is difficult to recommend one because all fourteen are different, though perhaps 103 and 202 particularly excel. Should you choose a suite, 401 with its private terrace will certainly not disappoint. What's more, in the centre of the hotel's gardens is a greenhouse containing the most astonishing variety of orchids.

Restaurants of all kinds are available in the Bay Area, and among them European cuisine is well-represented.

The innovative 'Chez Panisse', in nearby Berkeley and its chef Alice Waters are so famous that President Clinton made sure not to miss a visit. 'Azie' and 'Bacar' are equally highly-regarded.

All it takes is a mere fifteen minutes from the international airport to reach the 'only luxury hotel on the Los Angeles beach', so says the publicity.

Romantic and elegant, Shutters on the Beach is a wooden white-washed building that faces the ocean and practically has its feet in the water. In terms of architecture, it rather echoes the style of the southern Californian villas built in the '30s. In the hall, fireplaces, lithographs and original works of art are thoughtfully arranged to give the final touch to a hotel which lacks absolutely nothing.

The comfortable and quiet bedrooms, decorated in shades of white and blue, contain video recorders, large television and no fewer than three telephone lines. The beautiful suites offer the same style of decor, some having parquet floors and fireplaces.

Outside, you can take advantage of the balcony to 'people-watch' and enjoy the remarkable panorama of the Pacific. The clientele is mostly American and European and the staff make up for their lack of experience with their goodwill.

The only reservation is that the swimming pool is a bit small. But with the whole of the Pacific Ocean a few feet away, who cares?

facts
One Pico Boulevard, Ca
T 1 310 458 0030
F 1 310 458 4589
186 rooms and 12 suites.
Singles/Doubles:
From US$ 330 to 525
Suites: From US$ 750 to 2500
Tax: 12%
Plan: EP
Airport: 15 minutes

dining
One Pico: for American cuisine.
Pedals Café: Californian cuisine.

recreation
Swimming pool, fitness centre
and volleyball.
18-hole golf courses, tennis court
and water sports nearby.

additional
Concierge. 24-hour room service.
Dry-cleaning. Multilingual staff.
Business centre. Sauna. Massage.
Jacuzzis. Steam bath. Bicycle hire.

facts
28500 Overseas Highway, Fl
T 1 305 872 2524
F 1 305 872 4843
30 suites.
Suites: From US$ 450 to 2000
Tax: 11.5%. Service charge: 10%
Plan: EP
Airport: 45 Km

dining
The Great House: French and
Caribbean cuisine.

recreation
Swimming pool, fitness centre,
snorkelling, scuba-diving,
water sports and fishing.

additional
Spa. Sauna.
Massage. Jacuzzi.

It is difficult not to fall head over heels in love with the tiny, private Little Palm Island near the famous Key West
But you could hardly be blamed if you did: brillant white sand, a swimming pool with waterfall, particularly varied tropical
flora and fauna surrounding thirty small villas with thatched-roofs — all go to make up the 'ultimate in intimate' romantic
holidays. An earthly paradise for lovers of nature and water sports (fishing in particular), this resort is only accessible by boat
or plane.
All the suites enjoy views of the sea, private terraces, stylish British colonial furniture, air-conditioning and enormous beds
protected by mosquito nets.
Little Palm Island is more like a private club, and, like the best of them, it has a few rules for the benefit of its members: there
are neither telephones nor televisions in the rooms and children under the age of 16 are not allowed.
In the evenings, chef Adam Votaw prepares the most original and consistently brilliant French and Caribbean cuisine.
Don't miss Thursday nights when no fewer than six dishes are served.
A stay on this secluded island will certainly make an unforgettable holiday.

thedelano

Opened in 1995, the Delano was one of the pioneers of a concept that's widespread today, the 'boutique hotel'. The innovative Ian Schrager, creator of the Mondrian in Los Angeles and multiple hotels in New York and London, cleverly anticipated the tastes of modern travellers by inventing what might be called the 'urban resort'.

By employing the services of the best (Frenchmen Starck for the design and Troisgros for the cuisine), Schrager has brilliantly surpassed his objectives, for it has to be said that the Delano is a hugely successful and original enterprise. As soon as you step into the entrance, you will realise this place is like no other, perhaps one reason it draws such an international and particularly European clientele.

The bedrooms and bathrooms are minimalist, spotless and so entirely white that the only colours you'll find are provided by the flowers. Try to reserve one whose numbers end in '15' because they are larger than the others but cost the same.

The swimming pool is one of the most beautiful in the city and will delight music-loving swimmers (and water-loving musicians). Why? Because there's an underwater stereo system.

Finally, the hotel's 'Blue Door' restaurant, owned by Madonna, is among the best in Miami. If you'd rather dine outside, try 'Poet's Café', the city's current hotspot.

facts
1685 Collins Avenue, H
T 1 305 672 2000
F 1 305 532 0099
238 rooms and suites.
Singles/Doubles:
From US$ 195 to 450
Suites: From US$ 575 to 975
Plan: EP
Airport: 30 minutes

dining
Blue Door: for fine dining in an elegant setting.
The Brasserie: for meals all day.
The Blue Sea: new Asian fusion cuisine.
The Rose Bar: for cocktails.
Beach Bar & Grill: for quick lunches by the pool.

recreation
Heated swimming pool.
24-hour gymnasium, indoor and outdoor fitness training, extensive recreational water sports.
18-hole golf course and tennis nearby.

additional
24-hour room service and concierge. Shops. Video library. Portable telephones and computers upon request. Business centre. Massage. Meeting and banqueting facilities. Aromatherapy. Children's play area. Non-smoking rooms.

www.ianschragerhotels.com
united states miami
135

Fourseasonshualalai

One of the most recent Four Seasons creations makes you think of only one thing: that in this dream hotel there is only one season, an endless summer, where permanently blue skies melt into the Pacific.

The most astonishing characteristic of this resort that lacks practically nothing is its near invisibility. The entire complex seems to melt into its surroundings.

At the front desk, you hand your credit card as is customary, and in return are given a Hualalai cocktail (named for an extinct volcano) — an absolutely delicious mix of exotic fruits.

The bedrooms are full of all those little details that count. Beside the bath are salts that supposedly counteract jet lag (we'll leave it to you to decide) and slippers provided by your bed. The best are 103, 112, 902 and 911.

Fitness fans will be in heaven when they see the quality of the equipment on offer and are taken in hand (literally!) by Darry a former American football Iplayer.

Finally, in the middle of black lava, the Jack Nickalus-designed golf course will delight the most demanding of players.

On Waimea, go to 'Daniel Thiebaut' for his unique French-Asian cuisine.

facts
Kailua Kona, Hi
T 1 808 325 8000
F 1 808 325 8100
243 rooms and suites.
Singles/Doubles: From US$ 450
Tax: 11.17%
Plan: EP
Airport: 10 minutes

dining
Pahu'a: Hawaiian Fusion cuisine.
Beach Tree Bar & Grill:
for light meals.
Club Grill: Pacific club cuisine.

recreation
Five swimming pools, 18-hole golf course, eight tennis courts, fitness centre, water sports.

additional
24-hour concierge and room service.
Dry-cleaning service.
One hour pressing.
Multi-lingual staff. Spa.
Children's activities.

halekulani

facts
2199 Kalia Road, Hi
T 1 808 923 2311
F 1 808 926 8004
412 rooms and 44 suites.
Singles/Doubles:
From US$ 310 to 520
Suites: From US$ 700 to 4500
Tax: 11.4%
Plan: EP
Airport: 25 minutes

dining
La Mer: French quality cuisine
with Provençal influence.

Orchid: Al fresco restaurant with a
view of the beach.
House Without a Key: for dinner.

recreation
Swimming pool, fitness centre
and all water sports.
18-hole golf courses and tennis
nearby.

additional
Conference and banqueting rooms.
Concierge. 24-hour room service.
In-house laundry. Dry-cleaning.
Children's activities.

If you are absolutely set on staying in Honolulu, which these days has too much concrete and tarmac, you should find the right place to stay. Hotels of really high quality are scarce and, in general, overpriced.

Luckily, at one end of legendary Waikiki Beach is the Halekulani, the benchmark for all local hotels.

In this 'house befiting heaven' the rooms are in pale neutrals with dark wood furnishings and soft wool carpeting. In some, the panels of the closets between the bedrooms and bathrooms slide back, making possible to gaze at the famous Diamond Head during your soak.

The staff are known for their efficiency and discretion (for example, at reception you are escorted directly to your room to carry out the formalities in privacy).

Though by no means the island's largest, the Halekulani's swimming pool is lovely and one of the only places on Waikiki to enjoy the sun whilst escaping the crowds.

Finally, the hotel's best restaurant 'La Mer' serves outstanding French cuisine while the canvas walls of 'Orchids' roll up to allow fragrant ocean breezes to enhance the exotic seafood-based meals.

Fourseasonsmaui

Maui, one of the most beautiful Hawaiian islands where it's usually dry and the sun almost never fails to shine, is home to an imposing resort amid mountains, valleys, luxuriant forest and the Haleakala volcano. Located on the Southwest coast, the Four Seasons faces the ocean and one of the finest white sand beaches on the island.

The bedrooms are decorated in the chain's trademark colour scheme of creams, ivories and pastels and have lovely teak furniture and large balconies with good views. Try to book a room in the inner part of the U-shaped building, as some of the most thought-after ocean views are from the centre courtyard. As with all Four Seasons hotels, the bathrooms are enormous, in marble and some even have flowers and plants.

A grandiose swimming pool curves around the palm trees and at its centre plays an impressive fountain.

The hotel can also arrange sailboat excursions on which you can take dinner, enjoy the moonlight or sail to the Molokini marine nature reserve for snorkeling. The scuba diving is exceptional here and in winter, this part of the coast is home to hundreds of whales.

'Maui no ka oi' — Maui is the best.

facts
3900 Wailea Alanui, Wailea, Hi
T 1 808 874 8000
F 1 808 874 2244
304 rooms and 75 suites.
Singles/Doubles:
From US$ 310 to 705
Suites: From US$ 585 to 6200
Tax and service charge not included.
Plan: EP
Airport: 25 minutes

dining
The restaurants offer a choice
of international cuisine.

recreation
Swimming pools, two tennis courts,
tennis table, fitness centre, windsurfing,
scuba diving, water sports, fishing,
volleyball and croquet.
Six 18-hole golf courses
and extensive tennis centre nearby.

additional
Conference and meeting facilities.
24-hour room service and concierge.
Business center. service. Parking.
Boutiques. Hair stylist. Sauna.
Massage and spa services. Beach.
Children's programs. Excursions.

windsorcourthotel

facts
300 Gravier Street, La
1 504 523 6000
1 504 596 4513
267 rooms and 57 suites.
Singles/Doubles: From US$ 250
Suites: From US$ 340 to 675
Tax: 11%
Plan: EP
Airport: 20 minutes

dining
Grill Room: gastronomic cuisine.
The Polo Club Lounge:
for quick meals.
The Salon: for tea and cocktails.

recreation
Outdoor swimming pool
and fitness centre.
Tennis and squash nearby.

additional
Conference and banqueting
facilities. Concierge.
24-hour room service.
Multi-lingual staff.
Garage. Sauna.
Jacuzzis.

A few minutes from New Orleans' French quarter, you'll spot the modern architecture of the Windsor Court Hotel. Inside, however, you'll be surprised by the traditional English decor found throughout the building.

This theme extends to the art: Gainsboroughes and Reynoldses are among the superb collection of paintings complementing antiques from the seventeenth, eighteenth and nineteenth centuries. The bedrooms contain enormous four-poster beds, English wallpaper and traditional furniture. Suites offer reception rooms, fully-equipped kitchens, Italian marble bathrooms, telephones with three extension lines and spectacular views over the city and Mississippi River.

It may seem bizarre to stay in an 'English' hotel on a visit to New Orleans, but the city and the region are famous melting pots of sometimes incongruous cultures, so simply enjoy the contrasts.

The mix of the historic and the modern help to make this hotel one of the best in Louisiana and, indeed, the whole country. Its reputation is further strengthened by the acclaimed 'Grill Room', rated among the best three restaurants in the country.

In town, don't miss the famous restaurant 'Commander's Palace' which for 120 years has welcomed travellers from all over the world.

thepierre

New York can be an overwhelming experience, even if you've been many times before. But the Pierre is a reassuring landmark standing like a safe harbour for those tossed about on the Big Apple's concrete sea.

Located at the junction of Fifth Avenue and 61st Street, the hotel was founded in 1930 by Pierre Casalasco, whose intention was to create the atmosphere of a private club. He immediately found favour with the local community, perhaps due in part to the fact that the famous chef Escoffier practised his craft here. Six decades and seventy million dollars later, the Pierre has regained its status as the 'Grand European Lady' of the city.

After only a few minutes here, you are sure to be converted to a disciple of this trompe-l'œil and rococo temple. At the top end of the scale, you can choose between one of the thirteen well-named Grand Suites; all are decorated to perfection, with some boasting reception rooms in marble, others lounge terraces.

On the 41st floor, the sixteen-room apartment which used to belong to Lady Fairfax was sold in 1999 to a New York stockbroker for twenty-five million dollars.

For new restaurants in New York, try 'Az' for its wonderful food or 'Le Zinc' for its casual yet eclectic atmosphere.

facts
Fifth Avenue at 61st Street, Ny
T 1 212 838 8000
F 1 212 758 1615
149 rooms and 54 suites.
Singles/Doubles:
From US$ 430 to 895
Suites: From US$ 695 to 5050
Tax: 13.25%
Plan: EP
Airport: 20 minutes

dining
The Café Pierre: contemporary
French cuisine.

The Rotunda: for tea, cocktails
and light meals.
The Pierre Bar: for cocktails and music

recreation
Fitness centre.

additional
Meeting and banqueting facilities.
24-hour room service and concierge
Dry-cleaning service.
Multi-lingual staff. Business centre.
Foreign currency exchange.
Secretarial service. Massage.

acts
7 East 57th Street, Ny
1 212 758 5700
1 212 758 5711
09 rooms and 58 suites.
ingles/Doubles:
rom US$ 490 to 675
uites: From US$ 725
ax and service charge included.
lan: EP
irport: 30 minutes

dining
he 57 57: international cuisine.
ho Lobby Lounge: for dinner on
ne terrace.

recreation
Fitness centre.

additional
Meeting facilities.
24-hour room service, business
centre and concierge.
One hour pressing.
Multi-lingual staff.
Secretarial service. Parking.
Spa. Sauna.
Massage. Jacuzzis.

etween Park and Madison Avenues, as centrally and fashionably located as it is possible to be, Manhattan's largest hotel
as the very best views of the city. Among the most recent additions to the list of luxury hotels in New York, the Four
easons' modern and fascinating style was conceived by the renowned architect I.M Pei.

rom the large and impressive entrance hall, the subdued light barely reaches the front desk. The lobby stretches off into
he distance, marble is everywhere, sycamore mingles with steel and you can't help feeling that the interior are a bit cold
n spite of their obviously chic style.

he bedrooms boast no less than 550 square feet, and from the fastest-filling bathtub in town you can look out over Central Park.
or a once in a lifetime experience — for you and your bank manager — reserve the Presidential suite: it takes up almost
,000 square feet on the 52nd floor.

Jaturally, the staff are more than competent and will respond to your every wish. Devotees of Martinis will be interested
o know that the very chic bar of the hotel (57-57) offers fifteen different ways of serving their favourite drink.

he Four Seasons in New York is exactly what a hotel of the millennium should be.

twinFarms

Twin Farms is the most luxurious destination in the world if you like to stay in the countryside.

No expense has been spared to convert this 1795 house into a hotel, or, more precisely, the most costly little inn in the world.

Designed by Alan Wanzenberg, the famous New York architect, there are just four suites and nine cottages of various sizes. None are the same, but all are large and contain remarkable works of art (the largest boasts paintings by Stella and Hockney), sofas, fireplaces and enormous bathrooms with bathtubs the size of small swimming pools. Given all of this, it's difficult to recommend one over another, but when Bill Gates stayed he took 'The Studio' perhaps the height of seclusion and luxury. Even the Rockefellers are regular visitors; one stay here will tell you why. Twin Farms is so private it even has its own skating rink and ski slopes with lifts!

Lastly, if you have a few dollars in the bank, don't make life complicated — book the entire place for the reasonable sum of 14,500 dollars per day.

facts
Stage Coach Road, Vt
T 1 802 234 9999
F 1 802 234 9990
14 rooms and suites.
Singles/Doubles: From US$ 700
Tax and service charge included.
Plan: EP
Airport: 45 minutes

dining
The restaurant serves
superb gastronomic cuisine.

recreation
Tennis, croquet, fully equipped
fitness centre, fishing, hiking, biking
and skiing.

additional
24-hour room service.
Japanese furo.

facts
275 Main Street, Vt
T 1 802 496 6350
F 1 802 496 6354
9 rooms and 2 suites.
Singles/Doubles:
From US$ 300 to 550
Suites: From US$ 600
Tax: 9% Service charge: 10%
Plan: CP
Airport: 75 Km

dining
The restaurant proposes
contemporary American cooking
with regional influences.
Tea is served daily in the library.

recreation
Mountain-biking, hiking,
horseback riding, polo, hunting,
fishing, canoeing, kayaking, rafting,
skiing and flying club.

additional
Room Service. Full service day spa.
Meeting and banquet facilities.
Whirlpool.

Located in the Mad River Valley, the Pitcher Inn is a New-England style building with white clapboard siding, wide porches and a gabled rooftop. Inside, the atmosphere is as cozy and welcoming as a visit to your grandmother's — if your grandmother had exquisite taste, a flair for the whimsical and happened to be a gourmet chef, that is.

Nine large bedrooms are offered along with two two-bedroom suites in an adjacent barn. Each follows a theme specific to the state, such as trout fishing, mountaineering, and two Vermont-born U.S. presidents. In addition to massive furniture and creatively integrated memorabilia, all have well-hidden entertainment systems and computer and fax hook-ups. Most have wood burning fireplaces and Jacuzzis.

The 40-seat restaurant features seasonally-inspired dishes based on contemporary American cuisine and prepared with locally-farmed ingredients. Intimate dinners can also be set up in the wine cellar, home to an impressive 4,500 bottles.

Skiing, hiking and golf are just a few of the activities available in the surrounding countryside. And should you need an apres-ski or post-hike massage, the hotel can arrange this and other treatments at the day spa across the road.

Moreover, Warren's own authentic country store is the perfect place to stock up on everything from handicrafts to maple sirup.

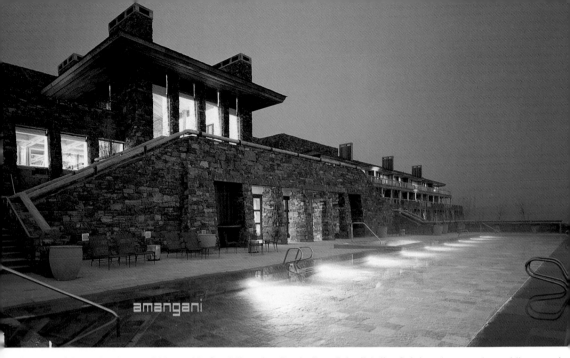

amangani

Amangani (meaning 'peaceful home' in Sanskrit and native Indian dialect) is the first American venture of the superb Amanresorts hotel group and shares the same pursuit of excellence as its sister properties in Asia.

In remarkably unspoilt Wyoming, in the middle of a thousand-acre ranch, the hotel sits 7,000 feet above sea level and is constructed entirely of materials such as cedar, Pacific redwood and Oklahoma sandstone.

The bedrooms follow the same natural theme and combine the minimalism of Zen style with rustic simplicity: all have redwood floors, enormous platform beds, superb bathrooms with deep tubs and balconies or terraces.

The very best views through the clear mountain air of the snow-capped Rockies are from the top-floor Grand Teton suite. Nature-lovers will be in their element: bison, for so long near to extinction, once again roam freely and eagles whirl and turn above.

At this very popular hotel (it's almost always fully-booked), the young and bright staff are especially energetic and helpful. In Jackson Hole, try 'Range' restaurant for local specialities.

facts
1535 North East Butte Road, Wy
T 1 307 734 7333
F 1 307 734 7332
40 suites.
Singles/Doubles:
From US$ 450 to 750
Tax: 6%. Service charge: 10%
Plan: EP
Airport: 15 minutes

dining
The Grill: for breakfast, lunch
and dinner.
The Granary: American cuisine.
Bar.

recreation
Swimming pool and health centre.
Tennis, riding and skiing nearby.

additional
24-hour room service.
Air-conditioning. Library. Excursions.

A twenty-storey vision in glass and marble, the Four Seasons Cairo's location gives it two important advantages. Not only is it the only hotel in Egypt offering views of the Great Pyramids and the Nile River, it is also blissfully free of the traffic noise and smog that can plague the rest of the city.

Upon entering, your bags will be whisked away while a staff member escorts you to the third-floor lobby for check-in. This level of personal service is impressive, but nothing compared to first sight of the magnificent, flower-filled lobby itself! Once in your room you will be put immediately at ease by the classic yet eclectic décor and pampering amenities. Splendid marble bathrooms feature separate showers and deep tubs perfect for a post-journey soak.

Eclecticism applies to the cuisine as well, inspired by Lebanese, Moroccan and Italian flavours and served in a contemporary dining room with views of the Nile.

Of course, every desert haven needs an oasis, and the Four Seasons has this covered in the form of its spa and wellness centre. The largest in Cairo, it offers swimming pool access, the latest exercise equipment and a full range of massage and skin-care treatments. Not a bad alternative to the mid-day Egyptian sun!

facts
35 Giza Street
Al Orman, Giza 12311
T 20 2 573 1212
F 20 2 568 1616
271 rooms and suites.
Singles/Doubles: From US$ 220 to 330
Suites: From US$ 550 to 4,000
Tax & Service charge: 20%
Plan: EP
Airport: 45 minutes

dining
Seasons restaurant serves a cuisine influenced by Mediterranean flavours. Poolside Bar and Grill.

Library Bar.
Tea Lounge & Lobby Bar.

recreation
Outdoor heated swimming pool, health/fitness facility.
18-hole golf course, tennis courts and horseback riding nearby.

additional
24-hour business services, room service & concierge. Spa and wellness centre. Jacuzzi/whirlpool. Massage. Hair Salon. Casino. Shopping Center. Meeting rooms. In-room fax, computer and Internet connection.

themenahouse

facts
Pyramids' Road
T 20 2 383 3222
F 20 2 383 7777
485 rooms and 13 suites.
Singles/Doubles:
From US$ 150 to 300
Suites: From US$ 660 to 1450
Tax: 7% Service charge: 12%
Plan: EP
Airport: 40 minutes

dining
Al Rubayyat: gourmet cuisine.
Khan el Khalili for international
cuisine.

Moghul Room for Indian cuisine.
The Greenery: for .continental cuisine
and breakfast.
Oasis: poolside restaurant for lunch.

recreation
Outdoor swimming pool, tennis
courts and a private 18-hole/two
fairway golf course at the base of
the Pyramids.

additional
24-hour room service. Concierge.
Fully-equipped Executive Centre.
Conference and banquet facilities.
Casino. Helipad. Night-club.

It isn't often one sleeps next door to one of the Seven Wonders of the World.
Just steps from the Pyramids of Giza, the Mena House began its life during the mid-nineteenth century as a royal hunting lodge.
Since becoming a grand hotel in 1869, it has hosted almost every politician, celebrity and member of royalty to visit Egypt.
This breathtaking Arabian palace is a fantasy of mosaic floors, brass-bound wooden doors and Islamic antiques,
complemented by every modern convenience (making it one of the only hotels in the world to offer full-blown computer
technology and camel riding). There have been a number of expansions over the years (mainly the addition of the garden
wing in 1976) but soul of the place remains the old wing with its classic Moorish style.
Garden wing rooms have balconies with views of the swimming pool, jasmine-scented gardens or Pyramids. However, the
old section is more atmospheric and its rooms have more panache. Among the suites, the 'Montgomery' (number 706)
and the 'Churchill' (number 632) are an especially fine choice thanks to their large terraces overlooking the Pyramids.
While the main attraction of the Mena House is obvious, you might also like to know that the hotel has a casino and the
only 18-hole golf course in Cairo.

theoberoi

You already know the French Riviera, the Italian Riviera — but the Egyptian Riviera?

One could hardly call Egypt's Red Sea Coast anything else, thanks to a recent influx of deluxe hotels and international holiday-makers who come for the sun, excellent beaches and some of the best diving in the world. A most welcome newcomer is courtesy of the Oberoi Group.

The Oberoi Sahl Hasheesh is set on a 450-metre private beachfront backed by rugged mountains. Inspired by Arabic Islamic architecture, its impressive domes, arches and columns create an exotic contrast to its seaside surroundings.

Guest accommodation comprises 104 ground-level suites, each with its own landscaped courtyard. Their decor is best described as nouveau Arabian — refined, uncluttered, but full of well-placed details such as Islamic-style furniture, Bedouin carpets and various objets d'art.

Meals based on seafood can be had at the main restaurant, while a more informal venue serves continental and Oriental cuisine. A large infinity edge pool, tennis courts and well-equipped exercise facility are on the grounds, though most of the recreation centres around the Beach Club, where snorkelling, sailing and windsurfing are among the possibilities.

facts
P.O Box 117, Red Sea
T 20 65 440 777
F 20 65 440 788
104 suites.
Singles/Doubles:
From US$ 250 to 1300
Tax: 8%. Service charge: 12%
Plan: EP
Airport: 20 minutes

dining
The seafood restaurant serves fine cuisine and features live entertainment. The dining room: for continental cuisine.

Al fresco meals can be enjoyed at the café overlooking the sea.

recreation
Swimming pool, tennis courts, fitness centre, windsurfing, sailing, health club and snorkelling.

additional
24-hour room service. Babysitting. Meeting facilities. Business center. Non-Smoking rooms.Beauty salon. Laundry and valet service. Shops. Children's facilities. Sauna. Massage. Library.

facts
P.O Box 90352 - Shanzu Beach
T 254 11 485 721
F 254 11 485 453
166 rooms and suites.
Singles/Doubles: From US$ 160
Suites: From US$ 220
Tax: 19%. Service charge: 10%
Plan: MAP
Airport: 30 Km

dining
Sokoni Plaza: coffee house with
Lamu theme.
Fountain Restaurant: breakfast
and lunch buffet.

Jahazi Grill: for seafood specialities.
Two bars for cocktails.

recreation
Swimming pool, four tennis courts,
squash courts, windsurfing,
scuba-diving, sailing, deep-sea
fishing, table tennis, volley-ball
and aerobics.

additional
24-hour room service. Conference and
banquet facilities. Business centre.
Boutiques. Fully air-conditioned.
Complimentary shuttle bus.
Babysitting. Excursions on request.

Set on a perfect beach facing the Indian Ocean and shaded by swaying palm trees, the Mombasa Serena Beach Hotel
offers a retreat that is soothing and stimulating at the same time.

Inspired by the thirteenth-century Swahili town of Lamu, the resort comprises of authentic flat-roofed buildings nestled
amidst bougainvillea-filled gardens and lush lawns. The rooms and suites, all decorated with native art and furniture, open
onto private ocean-view balconies or tranquil, tropical courtyards.

While there is no shortage of modern amenities, the hotel also offers many opportunities to experience the region's cultural
heritage. In addition to various entertainment choices, 'Swahili Evenings' follow the theme of a street fair and feature
demonstrations by local cooks and craftsmen.

Much of the Kenyan coastline is dedicated to preserving native marine life, so there are several reserves and parks nearby.
You might also take advantage of the hotel's prime location on beautiful Shanzu Beach for complimentary water sports
such as coral-reef snorkelling, scuba diving, windsurfing and deep-sea fishing. Sailing trips on native boats, or *dhows*, can
also be arranged. All in all, the Mombasa Serena is the quintessential getaway.

princemaurice

The Prince Maurice is the finest example of a new concept in Mauritian hotels — one that has moved away from over-decorated palaces toward a fresher and more relaxing plan of nature in harmony with simple decor.

Overlooking a peaceful lagoon and its coral barrier reef, the hotel's basic elements are marble, wood and stone.

Its outstanding architecture balances space and natural light to create an atmosphere of tranquillity, while interiors are understated yet welcoming with a hint of Asian influence.

Suites are scattered along the pristine beach, tucked into landscaped gardens, or even suspended over the lagoon itself. Those designated as Junior are anything but, considering their generous 750 square feet.

It is the Senior suites, however, that really excel in luxury. In addition to 1400 square feet, each has a large terrace and private swimming pool with stunning panoramic views.

Guests can choose from an all-inclusive menu of sports including snorkelling, water-skiing and windsurfing. Arrangements can be also be made for scuba diving, fly-fishing, or even a cruise.

facts
Choisy Road
T 230 413 91 00
F 230 413 91 29
88 suites.
Singles/Doubles: From US$ 350
Tax and service included.
Plan: CP
Airport: 45 minutes

dining
The restaurant serves international cuisine.

recreation
Swimming pools, tennis courts, fitness centre and all water-sports.

additional
24-hour room service. Concierge. Meeting and banquet facilities. Activities for children. Boutiques. Business centre. Hair stylist. Spa. Guerlain Imperial beauty centre.

facts
Royal Road
T 230 209 8300
F 230 263 8455
57 rooms and 27 suites.
Singles/Doubles:
From MUR 12 700 to 19 000
Suites: From MUR 37 000 to 78 000
Tax and service charge included.
Plan: EP
Airport: 60 minutes

dining
La Goélette and the Beach
Restaurant serve international
cuisine.

recreation
Swimming pool, putting green,
three tennis courts, squash court,
fitness centre, water-skiing,
water sports, fishing, billiards.
9-hole golf course nearby.

additional
24-hour room service. Private
limousine and helicopter service.
Boutiques. Duty free jewellery.
Beauty salon. Hair stylist. Babysitting.
Sauna. Massage. Jacuzzis.
Children's programs.
Casino and discotheque nearby.

Five hundred miles from Madagascar, Mauritius has the good fortune to host one of the most beautiful hotels In all the Indian Ocean: the Royal Palm. Principally constructed of stone, palm leaves and wood, the Royal Palm is located near to Grand Baie and, having its own lagoon, is ideal for water sports.

All the bedrooms, with tastefully decorated interiors, private balconies and terraces, look out over the sea.

But if you really want to splash out, the suites enjoy their own Jacuzzis and private staircases to the beach. The finest is the Royal, a true masterpiece.

As the clientele is mostly made up of families, nightlife is not the focus here. So, nightclubbers, if the hotel's band is not enough, plan to find your amusement elsewhere.

However, this familial atmosphere has not prevented the Royal Palm from counting among its guests Catherine Deneuve and Jacques Chirac. Indeed, many celebrities have taken advantage of Mauritius' remote location to indulge in a relaxed, friendly, away-from-it-all holiday.

The exceptional service cannot be praised too highly and is an integral part of the hotel's deserved success.

letouessrok

Proudly occupying a breathtaking site on the east coast of Mauritius, Le Touessrok is testament to understated luxury. Acclaimed as one of the most romantic hotels in the world, this unique resort enjoys an idyllic location with white beaches and turquoise waters throwing its imaginative architecture into dramatic relief. Linked by a wooden bridge to the tiny Ile aux Lièvres, where some of the rooms are situated, the resort is built in the style of a Mediterranean village.

A short ride away by boat lie two more islands dedicated to recreation: the Ile aux Cerfs, offering a full range of water sports, and private Island Ilot Mangénie for sunbathing and barbecue lunches.

Well-appointed rooms have incomparable sea views, while the suites are strewn along the private beaches of the main island. Spacious, air-conditioned and decorated in muted tropical shades, all come with a furnished terrace or balcony.

After sundown, the focus switches from sun and sports to dining and entertainment. In addition to restaurants offering a variety of world-class cuisines, there are performances with different musical themes such as jazz, gospel and Creole.

With all this to offer, many resorts would rest on their reputation and leave it at that.

Not Le Touessrok, whose Mauritian staff is perhaps its greatest asset. Enthusiastic and ultra-professional, *seven hundred* of them provide a level of service that is almost over the top.

facts
T 230 419 2451
F 230 419 2025
200 rooms and suites.
Singles/Doubles:
From US$ 340 to 1160
Suites: From US$ 400 to 3500
Plan: MAP
Tax included.
Airport: 55 minutes

dining
Les Paillotes:
for elegant fine dining.
Giramino:
authentic Italian cuisine.
Khazana: North Indian cuisine.
La Passerelle: for breakfast buffet
and themed evenings.

recreation
Swimming pools,
outdoor tennis courts,
volleyball, parasailing,
scuba diving and
sailing cruises.
9-hole golf nearby.

additional
24-hour room service.
Conference facilities.
Shopping arcade. Car hire.
Beauty salon. Massage.
Sauna. Hairdressing services.
Florist. Activities for children.
Executive car and helicopter
transfers. Babysitting.

lemuriaresort

Lemuria Resort is named after an idyllic lost civilisation said to have been located in what is now the Seychelles. Indeed, from the moment you set foot on this exceptional property you will feel that you have stepped into a dream.

Occupying more than two hundred acres on the northwest coast of Praslin, an island dedicated to preserving its natural habitat and the many species of birds that reside there, the resort itself is built into a granite hillside overlooking two beaches. Every effort was made to ensure that the Lemuria blend in with its surroundings. Your first taste of this is as you enter the main building, where a natural stream flows gently through the lobby, down the main staircase and toward a swimmable emerald lagoon.

A handful of thatch-roofed buildings contain the suites. Large and luxurious with an organic feel, their exotic wood furniture and detailing are offset by tones of beige and cream.

Guests benefit from complimentary activities including a fitness centre, tennis and many water sports. There is also a stunning 18-hole golf course (first of its kind in the Seychelles). Following the beaches, rolling valleys and palm groves, its views are unforgettable, especially from the tee of the 18th, a spectacular par 5.

facts
T 248 281 281
F 248 281 000
88 suites.
Singles/Doubles: From US$ 350
Tax and service included.
Plan: CP
Airport: 10 minutes

dining
The restaurant serves superb international cuisine.
Bars for cocktails.

recreation
Swimming pool, two tennis courts, 18-hole golf course, fitness centre, scuba diving and deep-sea fishing.

additional
24-hour room service. Boutiques. Activities for children. Hair stylist. Jacuzzi. Spa.

facts
76 Orange Street
T 27 21 423 1000
F 27 21 424 7472
149 rooms and 58 suites.
Singles/Doubles: From ZAR 2640
Service not included.
Plan: EP
Airport: 15 Km

dining
Oasis: for breakfast and lunch.
Cape Colony: modern South-
African cuisine for dinner.
Oasis al Fresco: for light meals by
the pool (seasonal).

recreation
Two outdoor heated swimming pools,
fitness centre and tennis court.
18-hole golf course nearby.

additional
Conference facilities.
Multilingual concierge.
Dry cleaning service.
Business facilities.
Fully air-conditioned. Boutiques.
Beauty salon. Hair stylist.

When the Mount Nelson Hotel opened its doors in 1899, it was immediately christened 'The London of South-Africa' thanks to its unequalled style.

Surrounded by a superb park and set In one of the most beautiful towns in the country, the rose-coloured four-storey building has been splendidly maintained — obviously with no expense spared by its owners.

Here, you'll find everything you've even hoped for in a hotel — including steak tartare for breakfast — the likes of which has welcomed almost every major figure to visit South Africa in the last hundred years.

The bedrooms, with firm but very comfortable beds, have extensive, natural light. All are highly recommended, but 231 in particular is very special for its 180° views of the gardens and the mountain.

The very professional staff will make it a pleasure to take tea in the Lounge, where Rudyard Kipling, Conan Doyle and Wiston Churchill, among others, used to relax.

If you're dining in town, then choose 'Buitenverwatching' for its magnificent views.

thewestcliff

In a residential suburb just fifteen minutes from the fashionable shopping district of Sandton, The Westcliff Hotel is without a doubt Johannesburg's most luxurious hotel.

The property comprises eight adjoining multi-coloured villas. Following the contours of a vertiginous hillside, surrounded by formal gardens and cobblestone paths, it creates the illusion of a Mediterranean village rising up out of the trees. Fountains bubble in the courtyards, blazes of bougainvillea tumble over trellises and pots of lavender adorn almost every balcony. Guest rooms are spacious and plush, decorated in natural tones and classic, elegant furnishings. Though it's difficult to pick a favourite, it must be said that room 105 with its private pool is pretty hard to beat.

When it comes to dining, the eighty-seat La Belle Terrasse is exactly that; perched high above the valley floor, its picture windows reveal sweeping vistas rivalled only by the superb international cuisine.

With so much to do in the area (museums, botanical gardens and wildlife parks are all nearby) you'll have no trouble staying happily occupied. But do set aside an afternoon to lounge by the Westcliff Hotel's fabulous borderless swimming pool. One of two on the grounds, it overlooks Johannesburg Zoological Gardens and the verdant Magaliesberg hills.

facts
67 Jan Smuts Avenue
T 27 11 646 24 00
F 27 11 646 35 00
96 rooms and 19 suites.
Singles/Doubles: From ZAR 1560
Suites: From ZAR 2395
Tax and service included
Plan: EP
Airport: 30 minutes

dining
La Belle Terrasse offers superb
international cuisine.
Conservatory Polo Lounge Bar:
for afternoon tea and drinks.

recreation
Outdoor swimming pools, tennis
court and fitness centre.
18-hole golf course nearby.

additional
24-hour room service.
Meeting and banquet facilities.
Concierge. Limousine service.
Business lounge. Parking.
Beauty salon.

facts
Phinda Private Game Reserve
Kwazulu - Natal
T 27 11 809 4300
F 27 11 809 4400
16 chalets.
Singles/Doubles: From US$ 475
Tax included.
Airport: 25 minutes

dining
In the reed-enclosed boma or
dining area overlooking an open
plain, you will savour flamboyant
cuisine infused with Pan-African flair.

recreation
Outdoor swimming pool.
Canoeing, scuba diving and
snorkeling nearby.

additional
Room service.
Air-conditioned rooms.
Bush walks and picnics.
River boat cruises. Excursions.

Need to really get away from it all? Escape the two-legged crowd for the quadruped and winged creatures of Phinda Forest Lodge. Situated in the 42,000-acre Phinda Private Game Reserve, this exclusive resort is acclaimed as South Africa's most responsible wildlife tourism project.

The stilted wooden chalets (built to allow smaller animals to roam underneath) house sixteen human habitats surrounded by glass, allowing for maximum viewing of the dense forest canopy and its four hundred species of birds. With furnishings and African details arranged with zen-like simplicity, each has a bedroom, lounge and spacious bathroom where no luxury has been overlooked.

Game drives in open vehicles are offered twice daily, in addition to guided bush walks and white rhino tracking on foot. Canoeing and riverboat cruises take place on the winding Mzinene River. And for those who wish to experience marine life as well, trips to the Maputaland coastline can be arranged for turtle-viewing, snorkelling or diving. Other activities include star-gazing trips, visits to a Zulu cultural village, and swimming.

Your day of adventure will wind down with evening cocktails, followed by a sumptuous dinner in the boma under the moonlight (or on your private deck if you prefer). And to top it all off, the simple pleasure of being lulled to sleep by the sounds of the living forest.

malamalagamereserve

Very near to Kruger National Park, Malamala is one of the world's most famous safari hotels. It is also one of the best.

One hour by plane from Johannesburg (the hotel has its own airstrip), the lodge overlooks the famous Sand river, where large numbers of animals come to drink. You could not wish for a better location; lions, leopards, chimpanzees, elephants, rhinoceros and many others will be as clear as day right before you.

There are several reasons for the success of this hotel.

First, there is the experience and professionalism of the guides (all of whom have been formally trained) who will lead you to some unforgettable moments in the bush. Then, there is the level of accommodation: twenty-five bedrooms offer comfort and luxury unequalled in this part of the world without losing the feel of a true safari adventure.

Each thatched-roof bungalow has air-conditioning (definitely not a luxury in this region), two bathrooms — which even have heated towel rails! — and uninterrupted views of the savannah. The highly qualified and omnipresent staff (there are three to each guest) will ensure that you want for nothing. Finally, you should not worry about being cut off from the rest of the world: the New York Times will already be waiting for you in your room when you wake up.

facts
P.O. Box 2575
T 27 11 789 2677
F 27 11 886 4382
25 rooms.
Singles/Doubles: From US$ 1,000
Tax included.
Plan: FAP
Airport: 60 minutes

dining
The restaurant offers the highest quality cuisine in elegant surroundings.

recreation
Safari.

additional
Room service. Dry-cleaning.

londolozigamereserve

facts
Sabi Sand Reserve
T 27 11 809 4300
F 27 11 809 4400
36 suites and chalets.
Singles/Doubles: From US$ 625
Tax included.
Plan: FAP
Airport: 5 minutes

dining
Each camp has its own restaurant offering South African and international cuisine of the highest quality.

recreation
Swimming pool and fitness centre.

additional
Helipad.
Safaris.

Meaning 'the protector of all living things' in Zulu, Londolozi is one of the finest game lodges in the world. Located in the northeast region of Mpumalanga, South Africa, it has more than 28,000 acres of savannah and no shortage of wildlife — most notably leopard and the rest of the 'Big Five'.

The lodge is composed of five camps, four of which (Founders, Pioneer, Bateleur and Tree) are located high above the Sand River's edge and provide impressive views. The fifth, Safari Lodge, is tucked away in its own private corner of the beautiful Londolozi property on a dry riverbed. With thatched roofs and ethnic influences, each room was created by local artisans and has a viewing deck that allows guests to admire the wildlife until dusk.

Watch the leopards from a 4-wheel drive, take photos of nature still untouched by civilisation, or enjoy a bush walk — nothing could be simpler thanks to the reserve's world-class guides.

Devotees of both nature and luxury, the owners understand the importance of certain conveniences after a day of excursions. Thus, the food served here is superb, and the silver cutlery, fine china and quality of service certainly make a startling contrast to one of the wildest regions in Africa.

sabisabi

On the banks of the Sabi River within one of South Africa's largest private game reserves, Sabi Sabi is devoted to the well-being of its surrounding habitat and wildlife — and that of its guests, too.

Three all-suite lodges are offered, each with its own distinct theme. The Salati, named for a rail line that ran through the property during the Gold Rush era, evokes the romance of the early 19th century. Railway memorabilia and period pieces are found throughout the guest quarters, which though fully air-conditioned still rely on oil lamps for evening light.

Overlooking a well-frequented waterhole, the Bush Lodge is more traditional, featuring African textiles and salvaged-wood carvings. Its specially-designed courtyards are an ideal place to see and hear any of the region's 350 bird species.

The brand-new Earth Lodge is architecturally sculpted into the ground itself, with elements of water, rock and wood extending the texture of the wild. Plunge pools in each suite, a nature spa and private art gallery add to the unique atmosphere.

Bush barbecues and beside roaring 'boma' fires are two settings in which to enjoy Sabi Sabi's exotic, extravagant meals (included in the tariff) and vintage South African wines. Also included — and most important — are the safaris. Extensively-trained guides lead guests on day and night Land Rover trips into the bush, all but ensuring a glimpse at the 'Big Five'.

facts
PO Box 52665
T 27 11 483 3939
F 27 11 483 3799
46 suites.
Suites: From ZAR 3700 to 4500
Tax and service charge included.
Plan: FAP
Airport: 120 minutes

dining
Exquisite cuisine is served three times a day.

recreation
Swimming pool, health/wellness centre, safaris.

additional
Fully equipped conference facilities. Air-conditioned rooms. Art galery. Boutique. Library. Telephone/Fax facilities.

kirawiracamp

facts
P.O. Box 2551
T 255 27 504 158
F 255 57 504 155
25 luxury tents.
Singles/Doubles: from US$ 600
Plan: FAP
Airport: 20 Km

dining
The chef uses local and fresh
produce to prepare the finest cuisine.

recreation
Swimming pool.

additional
Nature and bird walks.
Hot air balloon excursions.
Bush picnic lunches.
Massage and beauty treatments.
Resident naturalist. Safari.

What will most amaze you when you first reach Kirawira Camp Western Serengeti (owned by the Serena Group) is the striking contrast between the simplicity of your natural surroundings and the remarkable luxury of this unconventional hotel. After arriving at the private airstrip, your own butler will lead you to one of the lodge's twenty-five tents and unpack your suitcases. Meanwhile, you can discover the Victorian antique furniture, mahogany floors, four-poster beds and bathrooms laden with porcelain and gold. There's even a small terrace from which to watch the sunsets.

The cuisine offered in the dining tent is extraordinary. You can choose from the à la carte menu or order whatever dish you want — the chef will be happy to prepare it for you. Everything is served on magnificent Limoges porcelain; it's truly difficult to imagine such luxury in this part of the world.

The professionally-trained guides know their trade better than anyone. You'll realize this yourself when they lead you closer to lions and many other wild animals than you ever thought possible. Here, there are not only mere glimpses through binoculars at wildlife; more than any other place in the world, the Serengeti, whose animals far outnumber the human population, allows you to get close to nature in the most unforgettable way.

Just a twenty-minute boat trip from Zanzibar's mainland, Mnemba Island Lodge is an unspoilt paradise whose captivating marine life will make diving one of your holiday's main pleasures.

Mnemba Lodge simply consists of ten Zanzibari 'bandas' built with local materials (a mixture of palm trees, bamboo, coconut matting and thatch), all with private terraces and access to the beach - numbers 6 or 7 are ideal for families. Their informality is enchanting, even if there is no air-conditioning or hot water available before dark.

In the mornings, you wake with the sun and are brought delicious home-made cookies, wonderful coffee and excellent fruit juice in what certainly are the most chic bandas in the world. The food is Pan-African, prepared using the freshest, fruit and vegetables available from surroundings islands.

The lodge is operated by the well-known South African company, CCAfrica, who pride themselves on excellent levels of service.

What is there to do? Walk around the entire island (it takes about a half-hour) admire the numerous dolphins and turtles or gaze at the fleeting sunsets, which leave a clean blue evening sky. The sunset cruises on *dhows* are wonderful.

To convince yourself even further, note that Bill Gates has come here several times, accompanied by his doctor and sommelier!

facts
Mnemba Island
T 27 11 809 4300
F 27 11 809 4400
10 cottages.
Singles/Doubles: From US$ 525
Tax included.
Plan: FAP
Closed from April to May.
Airport: 80 minutes

dining
The restaurant offers seafood-based cuisine.

recreation
Windsurfing, deep-sea fishing, scuba-diving and water sports.

additional
Excursions. No telephones.

zanzibarserenainn

facts
Kelele Square, Stone Town
T 255 24 233 051
F 255 24 233 019
51 rooms.
Singles/Doubles: from US$ 165
Plan: CP
Airport: 25 minutes

dining
The restaurant serves a mix of
international and local cuisine.
Light lunches by the pool.
Mangapwani Beach Restaurant:
for seafood.

recreation
Outdoor swimming pool.
Water sports and fishing nearby.

additional
Room service. Conference facilities.
Business centre. Air-conditioning.
Satellite TV. Babysitting.
Valet parking.
Laundry. Excursions.
Private beach nearby.

Zanzibar, famous for its spices and very narrow, winding streets, is a truly unique and legendary island off Tanzania. Its long and fascinating history — its strategic position in the Indian Ocean made it a prize for every century's empires — have left it with a culture combining Arab, Asian, European and African influences.

The Zanzibar Serena Inn successfully reflects this remarkable cultural mix and is far from being just another soulless 'international' hotel. Set right beside the sea, it is ideally situated for exploring the whole island and has been completely renovated with no expense spared by the Serena Group who owns and manages it.

The hotel has fifty-one beautifully decorated rooms (number 51 is the best) as well as the island's best restaurant, serving traditional local and international dishes.

Twice a week, musicians play while you sit on a terrace and watch the sunset and the Mawahs, the traditional Zanzibari boats, silently sailing along the coast. What's more, the service is impeccable; the staff are resourceful and attentive, friendly yet professional.

In this languid and exotic place, the rest of the world seems very far away.

ngorongorocraterlodge

Tanzania's Ngorongoro Crater is one of the most fascinating wildlife havens on earth. Left by a volcanic eruption almost three million years ago, today the 19-kilometre caldera is home to 30,000 wild animals — including zebras, elephants and various large felines — who share its thriving forests, grasslands and lakes.

On the rim of this natural wonder is Ngorongoro Crater Lodge, three intimate camps of Maasai-inspired cottages perched on stilts. Designed to harmonise with its environment, the entire village of simple stone and thatch huts is barely visible from the crater floor. And right there is where primitive stops! Inside, antiques, gilded mirrors, Persian carpets and velvet bedspreads mix with carved Zanzibar panelling and African art and details to create an eclectic opulence that must be seen to be believed. Each cottage comes with a chandeliered bathroom and the services of a discreet private butler. What's more, glass windows in the bathroom, lounge and bedroom command awe-inspiring views of the landscape 500 metres below.

Delicious, Pan-African cuisine is served in the dining room or outdoors, where at night large bowls of fire lend a ceremonial atmosphere. Each of the camps has its own communal living area and viewing deck, while the "Maasai Market" sells crafts and souvenirs.

facts
Ngorongoro Crater
T 27 11 809 4300
F 27 11 809 4400
30 suites.
Singles/Doubles: From US$ 450
Plan: FAP
Service and game drives included.
Airport: 278 km

dining
Pan-African cuisine is served in the outdoor dining area or dining room.

additional
Room service. Private butler.
Laundry service. Game drives.
Excursions. Massage. Shop.
Special programs for children.
Telephone and e-mail facilities.

facts

Station Touristique Yasmine Hammamet
T 216 2 248 800
F 216 2 248 923
210 suites.
Singles/Doubles : From TND 220
Suites and Villas: From TND 460
Tax and service charge included.
Airport: 60 minutes

dining

Le Gourmet: French restaurant for elegant candlelight dinner.
IL Delfino: Italian dishes in a colorful setting.
Le Venus: for light healthy meals.
L'Olivier: for traditional Tunisian dishes.

La Topaze: for breakfast.
Piano Bar.

recreation

Freshwater swimming pool, indoor heated swimming pool, gymnasium, two tennis courts, thalassotherapy center and water sports in summer season.
Two 18-hole golf courses nearby.

additional

24-hour room service. Concierge. Conference facilities for up to 300 people. Business center. Night-club. Limousine service. Private beach. Sauna, hamman and massage.

Size matters or so it could be said of the Hasdrubal Hamammet, a distinctive resort located in Yasmine Hammamet on the Mediterranean coast of Tunis, only one-hour's drive from the airport.

Facing a private white sand beach, this Moorish-style enclave is dedicated to revitalising and de-stressing its guests. At its heart is an enormous, state-of-the-art thalassotherapy centre offering the best treatments in a stunning atmosphere. Within over 50 individual cabins, massages, musicotherapy and mineral oil treatments (among others) are provided for your utmost comfort.

The resort grounds cover almost 17 acres of gardens filled with hibiscus, bougainvillea and jasmine providing rich fragrances around the cascades and fountains. Featuring marble floors, fine wooden carvings and an extensive collection of paintings on its walls, the Hasdrubal comprises only suites. The 'Villa Salammbo', with its 1,542 square metres, is the largest in the world (look it up in the Guinness book). The others vary in size, from 65 to 135 square metres and are gracefully decorated, featuring large bathrooms and balconies overlooking the gardens or the sea. Finally, a word for the staff. Charming, efficient and courteous, they are always at the ready to fulfil your every wish.

Dubai, one of the small states of the United Arab Emirates, has recently become a fashionable destination for travellers. There are various reasons for this: it's only six hours by plane from Europe, it's superbly run and safe, there are wonderful beaches and, of course, the desert. Moreover, Dubai hosts a prestigious golf tournament on its excellent courses and an annual international cricket competition.

Last but certainly not least, it has one of the best hotels in the world: the Ritz-Carlton. Opened in September 1998, it has become a benchmark for all of the Middle-East.

Situated on Jumeirah Beach, the hotel has the same high standards as those of its sister properties elsewhere but with some local touches too: the building is ochre in colour, Moorish in style and a complete architectural and aesthetic success. Bedrooms 401, 501 and 502 are among the best — and all on the fifth or sixth floors are superb (on these floors, you'll have access to the 'Club Lounge' offering delicious sweet and savoury canapés and drinks 24-hours a day).

Finally, the service: from the doorman to the waiters, the babysitter to the concierges, it's hard to say who is the most kind or professional.

facts
Jumeirah Beach
T 971 4 399 4000
F 971 4 399 4001
138 rooms and suites.
Singles/Doubles: From US$ 400
Plan: EP
Airport: 30 minutes

dining
La Baie: gastronomic cuisine.
Splendido: Italian cuisine.
The Lobby lounge: for tea.
The Library: for cocktails.
Cascades: for lunch by the pool.

recreation
Two swimming pools, four tennis courts and two squash courts. Many 18-hole golf courses nearby.

additional
24-hour room service.
Meeting facilities.
Business services centre.
Full-scale spa. Massage.
Beauty services. Hydrotherapy.

pamushana

facts
Malilangwe Private Wildlife Reserve
T 263 4 722 983
F 263 4 735 530
6 villas.
Singles/Doubles: From US$ 480
Plan: FAP
Airport: 25 minutes

dining
The meals are served on al-fresco
dining deck overlooking the
Malilangwe Lake or in the
air-conditioned dining room.

recreation
Heated swimming pool,
fitness centre, fishing, canoeing,
game drives and walks.
18-hole golf course nearby.

additional
Sauna. Gift Boutique.
Library. Laundry.

Opened in 1998, Pamushana — 'place of sunshine' — sits atop a sandstone escarpment with spectacular panoramic views. This exclusive lodge is situated on the 105,000-acre Malilangwe Private Wildlife Reserve in the lesser-known southeast of Zimbabwe, adjacent to Gonarezhou National Park. The largest such reserve in Africa, it hosts a wide variety of animals including the 'Big Five' and some uncommon ones too.

Accommodating a maximum of 16 guests, Pamushana was built at a cost of almost six million dollars. Architects and decorators incorporated exotic works of art, richly-textured materials and furniture from all over Africa. Each of the six enormous villas features air-conditioning, a king-size bed, spacious bathroom, a telescope to admire the wildlife or night sky and, above all, a private swimming pool set in a gorgeous teak game viewing deck.

The restaurant offers first-rate, beautifully presented meals. And with nearly 7,000 bottles of wine in the cellar, there's little chance of dying of thirst!

Malilangwe is one of the few places in Africa the endangered black rhinoceros can be found. Furthermore, with over 400 species of birds and one of the highest concentrations of raptors in the world, the reserve is a haven for bird enthusiasts as well.

caribbean
mexico

cap|uluca

Cap Juluca is a Moroccan palace with one major difference — it's lost in the middle of the Caribbean on the still unspoilt island of Anguilla, facing Saint Martin.

The hotel is made up of a complex of buildings with domes and arches spread across almost 200 acres of land planted with palm trees, orchids and numerous varieties of flowers. Inside each of the 18 villas on the beach, the decor is Middle Eastern in style, with air-conditioning, a sofa, a four-poster bed and a splendid bathroom in Italian marble. Furthermore, all ninety rooms and suites have sea views, and some of them private terraces which can act as solariums if you have had enough of the beach (if that's even possible).

One of the hotel's main assets is the quality of the pure white and seemingly endless beaches (more than one mile long!) as well as the crystal clear water.

Sporting activities are very well-provided for and most, not surprisingly, centre on water sports.

By contrast, there is little in the way of nightlife and hectic socialising. In short, Cap Juluca is definitely the best place for those (particularly couples) who seek a quiet, undisturbed and civilised hideaway.

facts
P.O. Box 240
T 1 264 497 6666
F 1 264 497 6617
98 rooms and suites.
Singles/Doubles: From US$ 420
Tax: 8% Service: 10%
Plan: CP
Airport: 10 minutes

dining
Kemia: for international cuisine.
George's: French and North
American cuisine.

recreation
Swimming pool, fitness centre,
sailing, windsurfing, water-skiing,
scuba-diving, tennis and croquet.

additional
Room service.
Business and meeting facilities.
Children's activities. Library.
Boutiques. Massage.

facts

P.O.Box 173
T 264 497 6111
F 264 497 6011
Singles/Doubles:
From US$ 265 to 715
Suites: From US$ 440 to 2410
Plan: EP
Tax: 8%. Service charge: 10%
Closed in September and October
Airport: 20 minutes

dining

Head Chef Alain Laurent and his team provide the highest quality of superb French cuisine, touched with subtle Caribbean flavours.
Le Bistro offers casual lunches in a relaxed beachfront setting.

recreation

Three fresh water free form pools.
Fitness center. Snorkeling.
Four tennis courts. Water-skiing.
Windsurfing.

additional

24-hour room service. Concierge.
Meeting facilities. Library.
Children's activities. Boutique.
Hair and beauty treatments.
Heated Jacuzzi.

It's impossible to describe the appeal of Malliouhana in a few sentences, but we'll give it a try.

Location, location, location. On the Caribbean island of Anguilla, famous for its perfect climate, thirty-three dazzling beaches and refreshing lack of tourism. The resort is situated between two of those beaches, Meads Bay (voted seventh best in the world) and the very secluded Turtle Cove.

A room (or villa) of one's own. Fifty-five guest accommodations over twenty-five acres of lush tropical grounds. Elegant, mainly-white decor and enormous bathrooms. The Bougainvillea, a spectacular three-suite villa with its own pool and two Jacuzzis, can be booked piecemeal or as a unit. Incidentally, there are no TVs — but really, why would you need one?

Truffles, please. Directed by world-renowned chef Michel Rostang, the main restaurant offers the very best of French cuisine and service (ingredients from Paris arrive to be combined with island delicacies). A recipient of *Wine Spectator's* Grand Award, the cellar holds 25,000 bottles in 1,300 different varieties.

Life's a beach — and then some. Three freshwater swimming pools, complimentary water sports, tennis and exercise facilities. Children's activities include a climbable pirate ship, 60-foot water slide and Playstation games.

jumbybay

Minutes by ferry from Antigua, Jumby Bay was originally an ultra-exclusive sporting club whose annual fifty thousand dollar fee limited its membership to a privileged few.

Today it is a spectacular resort with its own privileged clientele. Recently renovated, this terrestrial paradise of palm trees, wild orchids and sparkling blue water is an exquisite hideaway promising rest, relaxation, and above all, total discretion.

Accommodation is provided in twenty-four suites and twelve villas situated throughout the grounds (where you will also find double hammocks hidden in the trees). Their elegant, breezy decor includes ceiling fans and mahogany furniture offset by colourful tropical prints. The villas feature private plunge pools and sweeping views of nearby Bird Island.

While water sports are limited to snorkelling, diving and water-skiing, the half square mile island is ideal for trekking and bicycling (except for golf carts, it is closed to motorised vehicles).

Gourmet European and West Indian cuisine is served in the Estate House, a two hundred and thirty-year old plantation manor. Here, as everywhere else in the resort, the staff is attentive beyond belief (while you're lounging on the beach, they'll bring you chilled towels!).

facts
PO Box 243
T 1 268 462 6000
F 1 268 462 6020
39 rooms.
Singles/Doubles: From US$ 650
Tax: 8,5%. Service charge: 10%
Plan: FAP
Airport: 10 minutes

dining
The Estate House is the hotel's signature restaurant.
The Verandah Beach Restaurant: for breakfast, lunch and light dinners.

recreation
Swimming pool, three tennis courts, fitness centre, putting green, croquet court and all water sports.

additional
Room service. Spa services. Massage. Activities for children.

facts
T 1 809 460 0300
F 1 809 460 0305
36 rooms and 9 suites.
Singles/Doubles:
From US$ 500 to 2000
Suites: From US$ 1300 to 2700
Tax: 8.5%. Service charge: 10%
Plan: AP
Open November to September.
Airport: 15 km

dining
First-class Mediterranean cuisine.

recreation
Swimming pool, 9-hole golf course,
two tennis courts, windsurfing,
deep-sea fishing, scuba-diving
and water-skiing.

additional
Satellite television. Game room.
Library. Massage.

The private property of the famous Italian couturier Krizia, the K Club doesn't seem like a hotel. It's more like a club for the jet-set — indeed, you reach the place after a fifteen-minute flight from Antigua on the hotel's private plane. Stretching along a three-mile beach, the resort is composed of a number of cottages, each a discreet distance from its neighbour, and was designed by the same architects of several of the hotels on Sardinia's Costa Smeralda. Each cottage benefits from a kitchen, direct beach access and the personal touch of the owner, who decorated the very large and beautiful rooms in pastel shades.

The K Club is very popular with film stars and royalty: during their visit, the Prince and Princess of Wales stayed in rooms 51 and 52.

Here, room service means that a chef comes to you in the morning to prepare breakfast on your private patio.

Every possible activity is provided for, but bear in mind that children under twelve are not usually allowed because the 'members' like their peace and quiet. In the mornings, the beach is so immaculate it's as if it was vacuumed overnight!

Bermuda, with its excellent climate, proper manners and immaculately manicured landscape, is the ideal choice for those who like their holidays with a dash of decorum. On one of its hilltops is the 25-acre estate known as Horizons and Cottages, whose atmosphere and service exemplify the island's genteel traditions.

Your initiation is via an enchanting manor house overlooking the South Shore. Traditional architectural details such as keystone corners, tray ceilings, and knee-high cedar fireplaces are reminders of the 18th century, when it was a grand plantation home.

Guests choose among nine rooms in the main house or thirteen cottages spread throughout the lush grounds. The cottages have private terraces overlooking the ocean, and most include a kitchen, where your rmaid prepares breakfast before bringing it to your bedroom.

Meals and teatime are events to be celebrated. Partake of the outstanding cuisine by candlelight on the Ocean Terrace during summer months, or by the dining room's open fireplaces in winter. A pleasant alternative is offered by sister properties Waterloo House and The Coral Beach Club, with whom the hotel has dine-around arrangements.

There is no beach, but guests are encouraged to enjoy the facilities of the Coral Beach & Tennis Club just across the road.

facts
Paget PGBX
T 1 441 236 0048
F 1 441 236 1981
45 rooms and 3 suites
Singles/Doubles:
From US$ 380 to 550
Suites: From US$ 510 to 770
Tax: 7,25% Service charge: 10%
Plan: MAP
Airport: 15 km

dining
The main restaurant serves exquisite cuisine for breakfast, lunch and dinner.

recreation
Swimming pool, 9-hole golf course, croquet lawn, putting green and tennis courts.
Fitness centre, squash courts, fishing, sailing, mountain-biking, horseback-riding and water-skiing nearby.

additional
Room service. Concierge. .
Meeting facilities. Children's activities.
Air-conditioned rooms.
Spa nearby.

facts
Hamilton HMBX
T 1 441 295 4480
F 1 441 295 2585
Singles/Doubles:
From US$ 198 to 440
Suites: From US$ 430 to 750
Plan: CP
Service Charge: 10%
Tax: 7.25%
Airport: 20 minutes

dining
Exquisite food is served in the hotel's
award-winning restaurant.

recreation
Swimming pool and fitness centre.
18-hole golf course, tennis courts,
sailing, boating, fishing, snorkeling,
squash and croquet nearby.

additional
Room service.
Banquet and meeting facilities.
Spa and private beach club nearby.

Just a three-minute walk from Hamilton, the heart of Waterloo House is a mansion that predates 1815, when it was renamed in honour of the defeat of Napoleon. Fresh flowers and soft music enhance its stately lounge, decorated with hand-printed chintzes, oil paintings and Georgian antiques.

Most of the equally-charming guestrooms are in the main house; some are in pink two-story buildings beside the patio. There are five private cottages, and one particular suite large enough for meetings or dinner parties

Terraced gardens scent the air and provide secluded nooks for reading or relaxation. But the showstopper is the large, wrought-iron terrace, where meals are served in nice weather and you can dance to jazz or calypso under the stars.

The hotel's dining room serves some of the best cuisine on the island. You will also have dining privileges at sister properties Horizons & Cottages and The Coral Beach Club. Be prepared to follow the dress code though (jacket and tie after six o'clock) and don't even think of those Bermuda shorts unless you have long socks to go with them!

A variety of water sports are available, picnic cruises on the property's launch provide views of Bermuda's outer islands, and the facilities at the nearby Coral Beach & Tennis Club are open to guests (transportation is provided).

At the western end of Bermuda, a fair distance from Hamilton, stands a uniquely charming hotel.

Closer in appearance to a holiday villa than a conventional hotel, Cambridge Beaches houses a complex of small, rosed-coloured pavilions. The main one dates back centuries and houses works of art, antiques and absolutely stunning English furniture.

Surrounded by five beaches, the small rose-coloured pavilions nestle within colourful, fragrant gardens and offer incomparable views over the ocean or the bay.

The atmosphere is friendly and relaxed, the staff polite and professional, and thanks to a superb chef, the cuisine is innovative and excellent. In the evenings, jackets are required in the hotel's restaurant, which keeps up traditional British standards.

In fact, this is one of the pleasures of Bermuda; it's a British colony maintaining the courtesies and elegance of another age, yet at the same time an exotic island with tiny beaches of pink sand, transparent water, stunning sunsets, and of course, the opposite of British weather.

An improvement: Cambridge Beaches now accepts credit cards. For years, it was one of the last that didn't.

facts
30 Kings Point Road
T 1 441 234 0331
F 1 441 234 3352
58 rooms and 24 suites.
Singles/Doubles: From US$ 515
Tax: 11.25%
Plan: MAP
Airport: 50 minutes

dining
The dining room serves
gastronomic cuisine.
Mangrove Bay Terrace:
for meals all day.

Pool Terrace: for lunch and dinner.
Daily barbecue by Long Bay beach.

recreation
Heated swimming pool, putting green,
tennis court, fitness centre,
water sports and croquet.

additional
Conference facilities.
Room service.
Spa. Marina.

facts
Petit Saint Vincent Resort
T 1 513 242 1333
F 1 513 242 6951
22 cottages.
Singles/Doubles: From US$ 770
Tax: 7%. Service charge: 10%
Plan: CP
Open November to August.
Airport: 20 minutes

dining
Al fresco restaurant overlooking
the harbour.
Buffet and barbecue.

recreation
Tennis court, fitness centre,
deep-sea fishing, scuba-diving,
water sports and sailing.

additional
Room service.

Petit Saint Vincent is truly a place apart.

Situated at the southern end of the Grenadines, surrounded by a crystalline, coral-filled sea, this tiny private place of 120 acres is uninhabited save for the hotel complex of 22 cottages, each with a living room, bedroom, bathroom — but no telephone. PSV really is a different kind of resort. An example? For service, you raise a yellow flag beside your cottage and a member of staff makes an immediate appearance.

On the other hand, if you want to be completely undisturbed, simply raise a red flag and you won't see a soul. Here, you have the privilege of absolute silence and seclusion.

Ask for cottage number one with its amazing views of Union Island, or number eight overlooking the Atlantic. In addition, if you want to feel like a true castaway, you can visit the atoll of Petit Saint Richardson (formerly Mopion), recently renamed by its owner, Haze Richardson.

Finally, it goes without saying that devotees of nightclubs and crowds would be rather disappointed by this unusual and enchanting resort.

halfmoonclub

Taking full advantage of its superb setting on one of Jamaica's finest crescent-shaped beaches, the Half Moon Club has played host to lucky travellers from around the world since 1954.

A string of Georgian colonial buildings spanning four hundred acres, the resort is a self-contained mini-universe on a bewildering scale: fifty-two swimming pools, seven bars, thirteen tennis courts, four squash courts, over forty-five shops and an 18-hole golf course!

If this wealth of recreational activities leaves you yearning for the quiet life, you can take a break in the peaceful guest quarters, which range from luxurious rooms to sea-front cottages with their own private pools to seven-bedroom fully-staffed villas stretching along a mile-long private beach.

Dining choices are no less extensive. Six different restaurants offer a wide variety of award-winning cuisines, including Italian, Asian and light meals from an authentic English pub.

Whether you're looking for a sport-filled vacation, an exotic meeting facility or simply a relaxing spot on the beach, in the Half Moon Club you will find a combination of them all.

facts
PO Box 80
T 1 876 953 2211
F 1 876 953 2615
418 rooms and suites
Singles/Doubles:
From US$ 120 to 245
Suites: From US$ 175 to 595
Plan: EP
Tax and service charge included.
Airport: 10 minutes

dining
Six restaurants offer international
specialities throughout the resort.

recreation
18-hole golf course,
tennis and squash courts,
fitness centre, volley-ball, badminton,
equestrian centre, deep-sea fishing,
water-skiing, scuba diving,
snorkelling, croquet court
and table tennis.

additional
24-hour room service.
Meeting rooms and banquet facilities.
Shopping arcade. Sauna. Massage.
Fully air-conditioned. Jacuzzi.
Facial and body clinic.
Activities for children.

facts
P.O. Box 64
T 1 876 956 7050
F 1 876 956 7505
114 rooms and suites.
Singles/Doubles:
From US$ 240 to 780
Tax and service charge included.
Plan: EP
Airport: 15 Km

dining
Round Hill: international cuisine
with a Jamaican influence.

recreation
Tennis courts, fitness centre,
windsurfing, scuba-diving,
water-skiing, water sports and fishing.
18- hole golf course nearby.

additional
Room service. Dry-cleaning service.
Foreign currency exchange.
'Bunty's cottage', the hotel's own
Spa offers beauty treatments, sauna
and massage.

Even with very stiff competition, Round Hill is one of the best hotels in Jamaica and certainly the best in Montego Bay.
For years a favoured winter destination of the likes of John F. Kennedy, Claudette Colbert, Grace Kelly and the Niarchos
family, today it remains an exclusive hideaway for discerning travellers.
Surrounded by a plantation and facing the Caribbean, the 'Pineapple House' comprises 36 deluxe sea view rooms.
But for something particularly special, choose one of the 27 private villas scattered throughout the tropical gardens.
Each has two, three or four suites with a private entrance, swimming pool and staff; the main building is easily accessible
by electric buggies.
Ralph Lauren was a consultant to Round Hill and contributed to its laid-back colonial elegance. He didn't have to travel
far to work, for his own private villa is close by.
Travellers looking for a simple and informal hotel should perhaps try elsewhere, for Round Hill is a sophisticated place
popular with the 'jet-set'.
The staff are extremely professional and experienced; little wonder, for some have served for over twenty years.

ritzcarltonjamaica

Framed by the Caribbean Sea and lush mountains of Montego Bay, the first Ritz-Carlton property to open in Jamaica is located on the island's north coast. Expansive but still offering the seclusion of a beachfront hideaway, it is set amidst the colourful gardens of a former plantation just minutes away from the city.

The hotel comprises a main pavilion and four separate guest wings in which arched doorways, vaulted ceilings, towering columns and open-air spaces are featured. Reflecting the style of Jamaica's historic plantation homes, its architecture is enhanced by traditional British colonial decor.

All of the 428 guest rooms and suites afford panoramic views of the sea or mountain countryside and contain all the traditional amenities of the Ritz-Carlton hotels throughout the world.

The list of available sports and occupations seems endless. To name just a few, you can shoot 18 holes on the stunning Robert Von Hagge-designed white witch golf course, dive to an underwater wonderland, play tennis or enjoy the facilities of the very comprehensive spa where a complete fitness centre, sauna and massage are available.

As for dining possibilities, a variety of different cuisines is offered throughout the resort. Whether you choose to indulge yourself or to enjoy light meals, there is a plate to suit every palate.

facts
Rose Hall Plantation
T1 876 953 2800
F1 876 953 2501
428 rooms and suites.
Singles/Doubles: From US$ 205
Suites: From US$ 275
Tax and service charge: 18.25%
Plan: EP
Airport: 10 minutes

dining
Horizon's: for breakfast, lunch and dinner.
Jasmine's: for a Jamaisian evening dining.
Seafood and Martinis: for dinner.
Cohabas: for afternoon tea and evening cocktails.
Mango's: poolside restaurant for meals all day.
The White Witch Club House: for breakfast, lunch and dinner.
The Rose Hall Beach Club: for casual lunch dining.

recreation
18-hole white witch golf course, swimming pools, tennis courts and fitness centre.
All water-sports are available nearby.

additional
24-hour room service.
Meeting and banquet facilities. Concierge. Multilingual staff.
Activities for children. Spa. Sauna. Massage. Whirlpool, Shops.

hotelitodesconocido

Ninety kilometers south of Puerto Vallarta, between the Pacific Ocean and Sierra Madre mountains, sits an enchanting hideaway known as Hotelito Desconocido.

Set on an estuary and sea turtle reserve, this environmentally sensitive resort relies only on natural sources for energy. That's right — there is no electricity! Illumination is provided by over one thousand candles lit every night, which only adds to the dramatic atmosphere. No need to worry about hot showers either; discreetly-hidden solar panels take care of that.

Hotelito Desconocido may blend calmly with its surroundings on the outside, but inside it's a different story. Colorful, eclectic local artwork is everywhere; some parts of the hotel, for instance the bar, resemble the elaborate shrines found in Mexican churches.

Thirty 'palafitos', or thatched-roof villas, hover over an idyllic lagoon, all with large private terraces. Following the same festive theme found in the public areas, they contain log canopy-beds veiled in mosquito netting, large bathrooms and open-air showers flanked with plants for privacy. Highly recommended are the Master Palafito Suites.

Nature spills over into the all-inclusive meals as well, prepared with the freshest local seafood, free-range poultry and resort-harvested produce. Even the most jaded traveller can't help but be seduced by Hotelito Desconocido's quiet and quirky charm.

facts
South of Puerto Vallarta
T 52 322 225 26
F 52 322 302 93
Singles/Doubles:
From US$344 to US$624
Suites from US$520 to US$780
Plan: FAP
Tax: 17%
All activities and service included.
Airport: 96 km

dining
El Cantarito: for dinner with an emphasis on fresh fish and seafood.
El Nopalito: for snacks and lunch.

recreation
Swimming pool, riding, boating, windsurfing, fishing, watersports and mountain biking.

additional
Jacuzzi. Spa. Massage. Helipad. Birdwatching and turtle nesting tours. Eological reserve.

facts
Av. Presidente Masaryk 201
Colonia Polanco
T 52 5 282 3100
F 52 5 282 3101
36 rooms and suites.
Singles/Doubles:
From US$195 to 265
Suites: From US$275 to 305
Tax: 17%
Plan: EP
Airport: 20 minutes

dining
Aura Restaurant offers contemporary
gourmet cuisine in a unique and
casual atmosphere.
Area Bar: for cocktails.

recreation
Swimming pool and fitness centre.
18-hole golf course nearby.

additional
24-hour room service. Business center.
Air conditioned rooms.
Non-smoking rooms available.
Meeting and banquet facilities.
Sauna. Jacuzzi. Spa.

If you think Mexico is one of the last places you'd find an ultra-chic boutique hotel, think again.

Floating in a frosted glass cube above a leafy boulevard in Mexico City's Polanco district, Hotel Habita epitomises the high style and state-of-the-art comfort twenty-first century travellers are looking for. Its minimalist design is a carefully-balanced mix of lines and curves, light and shade, with just enough colour to warm up the otherwise monochromatic public spaces. Sleek and elemental, the guest rooms feature traditionally-cool details like Eames chairs and crisp white bedding, and futuristically-cool equipment like flat screen TVs. Other forward-thinking extras include internet dataports, two in-house music channels and personal safes large enough to hold your laptop.

Aura restaurant offers contemporary gourmet cuisine in a casually artsy atmosphere. The rooftop Area Bar and Terrace, with its redwood deck and twelve-foot outdoor fireplace, is a great place to unwind by day or gaze upon the glittering skyline (and some well-heeled locals) by night.

The Habita's spa includes an outdoor heated pool (also on the roof), Jacuzzi and menu of soothing treatments that will make you forget you're in the heart of a cosmopolitan capital.

casanatalia

At the southernmost tip of the Baja Peninsula, where the Pacific Ocean meets the Sea of Cortes, the Los Cabos area is fast becoming *the* place to vacation in Mexico. In San Jose, *the* place to stay is Casa Natalia.

Owned and managed by expatriates Nathalie and Loic Tenoux, this 18-room hideaway crosses a European-style boutique hotel with an authentic Mexican home. Contemporary architecture and dramatic colours provide the edge — tropical flowers, trickling water and warm hospitality soften it just enough.

Each of the well-appointed guestrooms is themed after the region's spectacular deserts, mountains, clear skies and azure seas. Full of artefacts from throughout Mexico, all of them come with a terrace that overlooks the courtyard, gardens, pool, or fountains.

In the Mi Cocina restaurant, chef Margarita Pulido concocts delicious nouvelle Mexican-Euro cuisine highlighting local seafood, traditional Spanish ingredients and a few unconventional ones too. Dining on the terrace next to spot-lit palms, torches flickering in the breeze, you'd be hard-pressed to find a more romantic spot in town.

As for recreation, golfers will be in their element (the surrounding area is home to several Jack Nicklaus and Robert Trent Jones courses). Shoppers will enjoy wandering the quaint streets of San Jose and its interesting boutiques. And for those seeking something a little wilder, the lively Cabo San Lucas is a just a half-hour up the peninsula.

facts
Boulevard Mijares N. 4
Baja California Sur 23400
T 52 114 251 00
F 52 114 251 10
18 rooms and 2 suites.
Singles/Doubles:
From 180 to 200 US$
Suites: From 295 to 345 US$
Plan: EP
Airport: 6km

dining
Mi Cocina: for nouvelle
Mexican-Euro cuisine.
Palapa Bar: for cocktails.

recreation
Swimming pool.
18-hole golf course,
tennis courts, scuba diving
and surf nearby.

additional
Air-conditioned rooms.
Room service and concierge.
In-room spa services including
massage, manicure, facial and
pedicure. Excursions.

lasventanasalparaiso

Windows on Paradise — There's a name that could have easily been very pretentious. However, if you have the great luck to stay in this extraordinary hotel, you'll realise that its name, if anything is an understatement.

At the junction of the desert and the Pacific Ocean, at the southern most end of the Californian peninsula (but only an hour and a half by plane from Los Angeles), this immaculate two-story villa mixes Mexican and Mediterranean architecture.

What is most impressive is the level of elegance, thought and planning that have gone into its design. Every edge of the building, inside and out, is rounded and smooth; there is no sharp angle for the eye to catch on. This rare attention to the smallest detail enables the hotel to combine great luxury with the simplest Mexican motifs. In the enormous rooms (avoid, if possible, those on the garden) decorated with locally made furniture, there are marble bathrooms, video recorders and telescopes to admire the clearest of skies.

By the swimming pool, shaped like a snake winding its way along the villa, don't be surprised if your neighbour is a film star or a celebrity (the hotel is within easy reach of southern California).

facts
Km 19.5 Carretera
Transpeninsular
T 52 114 40 300
F 52 114 40 301
175 rooms and suites.
Singles/Doubles: From US$ 475
Tax and service charge not
included.
Plan: EP
Airport: 20 minutes

dining
The Sea Grill: fresh seafood
from Baja peninsula.
The Restaurant: regional
specialities.
Spa Juice Bar: for cocktails.

recreation
Swimming pools, tennis,
fitness centre, riding
and jogging.
18-hole golf course nearby.

additional
24-hour room service. Spa.
Desert excursions. Beach.
Whale watching tours.

Fourseasonsnevis

Nevis, the smaller twin of Saint Kitts, is a fortunate place indeed —it is here that the Four Seasons group decided to build its only hotel in the Caribbean.

Although it has quite an imposing design, the architect has succeeded in making the hotel's buildings melt into their natural surroundings, thanks to the extensive use of local materials and woods. The result is an exquisite blend of Caribbean and modern influences in the bedrooms and villas. The latter, next to the fairway, are particularly attractive and although recently-built they have already become very much sought after. Others are also highly recommended, notably the ten with views of the sea and the two overlooking Mount Nevis and the golf course designed by Robert Trent Jones II.

As to sports: on the long Pinney Beach, every variety of water sport is available. For the brave, excursions to Mount Nevis are organised, but remember that it takes nearly five hours to reach the summit.

While parents are busy enjoying themselves, children are kept happy with a programme of activities arranged by the hotel. Finally, the staff are highly professional (they memorise your name in a flash) and are always ready to please.

facts
P.O. Box 565, Pinney's Beach
T 1 869 469 1111
F 1 869 469 1085
179 rooms and 17 suites.
Singles/Doubles:
From US$ 575 to 625
Tax and service charge included.
Plan: EP
Airport: 10 minutes

dining
The restaurant serves excellent international cuisine.
The Cabana: for lunch next to the pool.

recreation
Two swimming pools, fitness centre, 18-hole golf course, windsurfing, ten tennis courts, scuba-diving, water sports and fishing.

additional
Meeting facilities.
24-hour room service.
Secretarial service.
Boutiques. Sauna. Jacuzzis.
Children's activities. Beach.

hotelguanahani

facts
Anse de Grand Cul de Sac
T 590 276 660
F 590 277 070
75 rooms and suites.
Singles/Doubles:
From US$ 290 to 950
Suites: From US$ 590 to 1650
Tax and service charge included.
Plan: CP
Airport 10 minutes

dining
Bartolomeo: Continental cuisine.
L'indigo: for breakfast and lunch.

recreation
Two swimming pools, windsurfing,
two tennis courts, scuba-diving,
water-skiing and fishing.
Non-motorised sports free of charge.

additional
Meeting facilities. Concierge.
Room service. Boutiques.
Laundry and dry-cleaning service.
Hair stylist. Massage.
Beauty salon.

In Saint Barthelemy, ten minutes by plane from its neighbour Saint Martin, the Guanahani combines original and charming Caribbean architecture with French rigour and sophistication.

With seventy-five rooms nestling amid fifteen acres of luxuriant gardens, the complex is one of the island's most important in size and the quality of its service. A blaze of colours (flamboyant rose-reds, lively yellows, loud violets and azure blues) characterise the interiors and exteriors of the bungalows which house the bedrooms.

With Gustavian-style furniture in pastel tones, air-conditioning and private terraces, all of them are different: some are rather more simple than others, but most overlook the sea.

Among them, the best are a step from the beach (bedrooms 52 to 57). The majority of the suites have swimming pools or jacuzzis; number 2 is really outstanding.

You have a choice between two white sand beaches, one looking out over calm waters protected by the bay, the other bordering a coconut plantation.

In the island's capital, Gustavia, be sure to reserve a table at 'Maya', a small, beautiful restaurant on the beach.

parrotcay

The owners of the very fashionable Parrot Cay describe their resort as 'the ultimate in chic simplicity'. They have achieved their bold aim by mixing the best of the Caribbean with a certain Oriental style.

Located in the northern part of North Caicos — half an hour from the capital Providenciales, Parrot Cay will undoubtedly delight anyone who loves seclusion, nature and moon-lit and starry nights.

Managed by Christina Ong and Keith Hobbes (who have already made their mark in Europe), the hotel has a chic and relaxed atmosphere with a mostly European clientele.

The bedrooms are decorated very simply: sisal rugs and white walls surround large, teak beds draped with white, muslin curtains. Each leads onto a terrace from which you can take in the most splendid ocean views. Parrot Cay has a main building as well as luxurious beachfront villas. If you decide to take any one of the latter, you'll be guaranteed the utmost privacy and peace for the whole of your stay.

The recently opened spa, the Shambhala, has already won itself quite a reputation in the area with its comprehensive healthcare including Thai and Chinese massages given by true professionals.

facts
P.O. Box 143
T 1 649 946 7788
F 1 649 946 7789
60 rooms and suites.
Singles/Doubles:
From US$ 250 to 3220
Plan: CP
Tax: 9%. Service charge: 10%
Closed in September.
Airport: 30 minutes

dining
Gourmet restaurant.
Poolside restaurant and grill.

recreation
Tennis courts, fitness centre,
swimming pool, scuba-diving,
water sports and fishing.

additional
Room service.
Book, video and CD library.
TV and VCR on request.
Spa. Massage. Boutiques.
Yoga classes.

facts
P.O. Box 70
T 1 284 495 5555
F 1 284 495 5661
98 rooms and suites.
Singles/Doubles: From US$ 480
Suites: From US$ 500 to 1150
Tax: 7%. Service charge: 5%
Plan: EP
Airport: 10 minutes

dining
The Sugar Mill: Mediterranean
cuisine with Italian touch.
The Pavillon for seafood specialities.
The Beach Grill: for lunch.

recreation
Seven tennis courts,
fitness centre, scuba-diving,
jet-ski, deep-sea fishing
and water sports.

additional
Children's activities.
Massage.
Excursions.

It was originally Laurence Rockefeller who, thirty five years ago, had the idea of creating a secluded and luxurious resort hotel among unspoilt natural surroundings. He chose an uninhabited bay whose half-moon shaped white beach divides forests from crystal-clear blue water.

Little Dix Bay comprises small pavilions which are placed around the rim of the bay, so as to give guests the best possible views.

The recently renovated bedrooms and suites seem like an extension of nature with their vivid, tropical colours, native wood and stone. All of them feature fieldstone walls, tiled floors, bamboo, wicker furniture, cast iron and overhead fans (air-conditioning is only available in certain rooms). There is also a little path leading down to the sea.

In the evenings, there is nothing better than simply relaxing on the terrace, cocktail in hand, experiencing the stunning sunset giving way to the clear, starry night and the scent of a dozen types of flowers. During the day, you can be equally active or, on the other hand, let the staff pack you a superb picnic lunch so that you can go off and explore the island.

madisonresort

It's been said that opposites attract. It can also be said that when blended correctly, they enhance each other.

Such is the case throughout Uruguay's Madison Resort. Set among sandy hills and euculyptus groves next to the Rio de la Plata (and just twenty minutes by plane from Buenos Aires), its architecture and interiors are an exquisite example of what can happen when east meets west, or more specifically, Asia meets Latin America.

Twenty bungalows and twenty-four Duplex Suites are furnished to reflect the simple beauty of the surrounding landscape. Stone floors, rich wood panelling, Asian antiques and indigenous textiles contribute to their stylish yet natural atmosphere.

When it comes to dining, the dramatic 'Pura' — meaning temple — is just that. Here you can enjoy inventive cuisine mixing oriental and occidental flavours in the sensual dining room next to a candlelit indoor pond, or outside on the terrace with views of the pool.

Another place where the emphasis is on balance is the Asian-style spa. In addition to a fully-equipped gym, sauna and meditation rooms, it offers a range of soothing treatments from hydrotherapy to massage with herbal oils.

Other diversions include a double cascade swimming pool, tennis courts and riding or windsurfing a short distance away. But perhaps the best is the Madison's new par 72, 18-hole golf course. Designed by experts for experts, it is one of the most spectacular in South America.

facts
Ruta 21, km 262. Dpto de Colonia.
T 598 542 9000
F 598 542 9999
44 suites
Suites: From US$ 250 to 330
Tax: 14%
Plan: CP
Airport: 1 Km

dining
Pura: for pan-Asian, western and local cuisine.
Mandara Bar: for private dining and for drinks.
The Shiva Lounge: for snacks, coffee and afternoon tea.

recreation
Swimming pool, horseriding, 18-hole golf course, fitness center, tennis courts, kayaking, windsurfing, sailing and fishing.

additional
24-hour room service.
Meeting facilities.
Non allergic foam pillows.
In-room CD player.
Housekeeping service.
Fax machines available.
Internet connection.
Beauty Salon. Free access to the Spa with hydrotherapy and body treatments.
Children's activities.

pacific

thekirketon

If there were ever any doubt, Sydney's successful hosting of the 2000 Olympics sealed its reputation as one of the friendliest and most happening cities on the planet. These same qualities describe The Kirketon, whose perfect balance of style and substance has garnered rave reviews from the international press including *Vogue* and *Wallpaper*.

The interiors of this early 20th-century building were redone by Australian designer Iain Halliday, who transformed the place into a temple of trendy. An overgrown toadstool lampshade by the front door, sleek white 1950s chairs in the lobby, a 'funhouse' hall of mirrors — all will be appreciated by devotees of what is high-class and hip.

Forty guestrooms in different categories are similar in layout and feature ultra-modern furniture, mirrored bedheads standing in for dime-a-dozen hotel art, VCRs, CD players and data ports. Homier touches are found in the details: mohair throw rugs, down pillows, the finest cotton bed linens, and something one doesn't see enough of in city hotels, windows that open.

Here you'll be right in the heart of Darlinghurst, Sydney's answer to SoHo, and a five-minute walk from everything else. See-and-be-seen types need go no further than the ground floor though, which houses two popular boutique bars and what the *Sydney Morning Herald* called the best new restaurant of 2000.

facts
229 Darlinghurst Road
T 61 2 9332 2011
F 61 2 9332 2499
40 rooms.
From: $AU 220 to 365
Tax included.
Plan: EP
Airport: 15 minutes.

dining
Salt: for international cuisine in modern, elegant surroundings.
The Champagne Bar: for cocktails.
Fix Bar: for cocktails and lights meals in a 'boutique' style bar.

recreation
Complimentary access to gymnasium, 18-hole golf course and tennis courts nearby.

additional
Non-smoking rooms available.
Fully equipped conference and meeting room. Room service.
24-hour reception and concierge.
Internet and secretarial services available. Multilingual team.
Parking.

facts
267 Darlinghurst Road
T 61 2 9331 1000
F 61 2 9380 6901
18 rooms and suites.
Singles/Doubles:
From $AU 270 to 385
Tax included.
Plan: EP
Airport: 15 minutes

dining
In-room dining.

recreation
Complimentary access to
gymnasium, 18-hole golf course
and tennis courts nearby.

additional
24-hour reception and room service.
Concierge. Multi lingual team.
Business and Internet facilities.
Laundry and dry cleaning service.
Air conditioned rooms.
Non Smoking rooms.
Parking.

In the heart of Sydney's Darlinghurst district is the Hotel Medusa, a stately Victorian building with a decidedly modernist soul. Opened in 1998, this Medusa's legend is one of beauty, drama and a dash of the unexpected. From the arresting pink and red lobby to the beguiling courtyard reflecting pool and some of the daring colour pairings (tangerine and royal blue, for instance) found in the 18 guestrooms, the accent is on sensual — and sensational.

The hotel is the brainchild of Terry and Robert Schwamberg, also responsible for The Kirketon just a few doors down. Their motto? 'To know what is important to the new generation of global traveller.' Luxurious, stylish rooms with large beds, designer furniture, ambient lighting and all the hook-ups you need. A big plus are kitchenettes (the hotel has no restaurant, but many neighbourhood eateries deliver meals the staff will gladly set up in your room). Moreover, The Medusa is Sydney's only luxury hotel offering an Information Technology room.

Maybe not so important, but pretty cool anyway, is the hotel's policy toward dogs. Not only are they welcome in the courtyard rooms, but doggy room service items are available along with a booklet listing points of canine interest such as nearby parks and fire hydrants. Is it any wonder The Medusa was named one Condé Nast Traveller's '21 Hip Hotels for the 21st Century'?

James Bond himself would definitely feel at home in this resort resembling a spectacular set from one of his films.

Hayman Island may be a celebrated meeting place for Australia and the world's famous, but here all visitors are treated as honoured guests by the very efficient staff. The hotel is regularly ranked among the best in every category, not least because of its location near the Great Barrier Reef, its luxuriant flora and fauna and transparent sea lapping the white sand beaches. The mission to relax begins with champagne (unfortunately, it's not Dom Perignom 1957) on the boat taking you from Hamilton airport to the island.

The bedrooms and suites — from which you can admire the most stunning sunsets and the remote islands — follow a variety of different styles. But whether you choose Japanese, Californian, Italian, Moroccan or Art Deco (perhaps the most beautiful), you'll find all of them create a relaxed and informal atmosphere in the most elegant surroundings.

If you think staying on an island means that there is little to do, you'd be wrong. The sports activities are numerous (especially when it comes to the water) and if you're not so energetic, you can always indulge yourself in the hotel's restaurants offering many different styles of cuisine. You only live once, right?

facts
Great Barrier Reef, Queensland
T 61 7 4940 1234
F 61 7 4940 1567
170 rooms and 44 suites.
Singles/Doubles: From AU$ 490
Suites: From AU$ 1300 to 3300
Tax and service charge included.
Plan: CP
Airport: 60 minutes

dining
La Fontaine: French cuisine.
La Trattoria: Italian cuisine.
Planters: Australian and Polynesian cuisine.
Oriental: Asian cuisine.
Coffee House: for meals all day.

recreation
Sea and fresh water swimming pools, putting green, tennis courts, squash courts, table tennis, gymnasium, diving, water sports, sailing, fishing, badminton, billiards.

additional
Conference facilities. Concierge. 24-hour room service. Boutiques. Beauty salon. Nightclub. Florist. Spa. Sauna. Jacuzzi. Children's activities. Extensive wine cellar.

facts
89-113 Kent Street
T 61 2 9256 2222
F 61 2 9256 2233
79 rooms and 21 suites.
Singles/Doubles:
From AU$ 460 to 540
Suites: From AU$ 670 to 1650
Tax and service charge included.
Plan: EP
Airport: 25 Km

dining
Galileo: Australian cuisine with a
dash of Italian.
The Orient: Australian and Asian
specialities.

recreation
Swimming pool, tennis court
and gymnasium.

additional
Conference facilities.
Business centre.
Spa. Sauna. Steam bath.
Children's activities.

A short distance from Sydney's financial district and famous opera house stands the Observatory, a grand neo-Georgian building bursting with a stylish mix of Australian antiques, period tapestries and paintings.

Often compared to the Cipriani in Venice (certainly thanks to the reputation of its restaurant), this hotel is *the* place to stay in Sydney.

The bedrooms are charming, with sash windows and subdued lighting. In each one, you'll find a VCR, CD-player, fax machine and telephones with no fewer than four lines. Some even have their own beautiful terraces.

But the finest achievement is the bathrooms: large and well-appointed, it is said that their showers are the best in the world.

There aren't many reasons, therefore, to take a suite. But if you prefer one, then ask for the very British 'Observatory Suite' with its outstanding attention to detail.

Style and elegance are not confined to the upper floors. Below ground, the enormous and imaginatively-designed indoor swimming pool is an unforgettable place in which to linger.

Lastly, for dining outside the hotel with the best view of Rose Bay harbour, make a reservation at 'Pier'.

turtleisland

Those seeking short holidays should not bother with Turtle Island.

If you would only spend a weekend, it's not the place for you. Who would stay fewer than six nights (the minimum allowed) after a journey of more than 24 hours from Europe?

The 500-acre island is owned by a wealthy American (Richard to his friends) who, about twenty years ago, sought a small corner of paradise for himself. Having found it, he agreed to share, but only with a select group of guests. That's why a maximum of only fourteen couples arrive by seaplane after a stop-over at Nadi, the nearest town.

The fourteen bungalows ('bures') are large, with four-poster beds, hand-crafted furniture and great bathrooms (there are two per bedroom). The beauty of the island is quite breathtaking and the sea is clear enough to amaze even the most blasé of travellers.

Any one of fourteen completely private beaches can be reserved for your personal use. The staff will prepare a marvellous picnic that you can take with you to your private beach or have delivered at lunchtime.

Once a week, there are boat excursions to equally beautiful neighbouring islands. A truly unique place.

facts
Yasawa Islands
T 61 3 961 81 100
F 61 3 961 81 199
14 cottages.
Singles/Doubles:
From US$ 540 to US$ 650
Tax and service charge not included.
Plan: FAP
Airport: 25 minutes

dining
The restaurant: for lunch and dinner out-doors.

recreation
Windsurfing, riding, scuba-diving, volley-ball and deep-sea fishing.

additional
Boutique. No television. Children's activities. Nursery. Excursions. Sunset cruises. Traditional weddings.

facts
Huka Falls Road
T 64 7 378 5791
F 64 7 378 0427
20 rooms and 1 cottage.
Doubles: From NZ$ 535
Tax: 12.5%
Plan: FAP
Airport: 10 Km

dining
The lodge dining room offers
international cuisine and a number
of special private dining locations.

recreation
Tennis court, sailing, fishing,
horse riding, petanque court,
rafting and hunting.
18-hole golf course nearby.

additional
Jacuzzi. Helipad.

When Huka Lodge opened sixty years ago it was a simple meeting place for fishermen owned and operated by Irishman Alan Pye, who was himself fanatical about fishing.

Today, it is famous the world over as New Zealand's finest lodge and a refuge for royalty and celebrities alike. It is also very exclusive: there are only a handful of rooms and suites at this little paradise set on the banks of the Waikato river (the largest in the country), amid acres of lawns and gardens. All of them offer an ambience of tranquillity and intimacy. The hotel prides itself on the quality of its cuisine. From breakfasts to candle-lit dinners prepared with the freshest produce, you won't find finer cooking anywhere in New Zealand.

In the evenings the atmosphere is friendly and relaxed, with guests chatting about the day's fishing on Lake Taupo, said to have the best trout fishing in the world. Of course, there is more to try. Surrounding the resort are miles of unspoilt countryside and mountains perfect for hiking and skiing.

The extremely professional staff provide faultless service and must be a source of pride to Alexander van Heeren, the Dutch proprietor.

hotelborabora

Two hundred and thirty kilometres from Tahiti, in the Bay of Pofai, is a superb resort surrounded by a sapphire blue lagoon. Even the most seasoned of travellers will feel they have discovered something entirely new when they first arrive at the hotel Bora Bora.

What sets this place so apart are the bungalows. Some seem to float above the stunningly clear water, others are in the middle of tropical gardens or on the beach. Choose one of the latter — in particular one of the eight with their own private swimming pools — rather than those directly on the lagoon (they may look the most romantic, but can be a bit noisy when the wind blows). Inside, there is no television; simply lots of flowers, the colours of the Pacific and furnishings of refinement and good taste. The bathrooms are magnificently decorated and the vast beds, surrounded by mosquito nets, stand beneath enormous fans.

Boredom is often cited by some as to why they would rather not stay on a small, tropical island. But here there are numerous activities, including some of the best scuba-diving anywhere. Of course, you can simply lay in your hammock, and rock the afternoon away...

facts
Point Raititi, Nunue
T 689 604 460
F 689 604 466
54 bungalows.
Singles/Doubles:
From XPF 45 000 to 78000
Tax: 8%
Plan: EP
Airport: 20 minutes

dining
Matira Terrasse restaurant: for breakfast and dinner al fresco.
Pofai Beach Bar: for light meals.

Barbecue on the beach every Wednesday.
Polynesian buffet brunch every Sunday.

recreation
Tennis courts, deep-sea fishing, scuba-diving, water-skiing, sailing, jet-skis, volleyball, billiards, basketball, riding and parasailing.

additional
Foreign currency exchange.
Boutiques. Babysitting.
Excursions. Video library.

emotions

SOFITEL
ACCOR HOTELS & RESORTS

Polynesia

5 paradise resorts in Polynesia : Sofitel Maeva Beach, Tahiti - Sofitel Heiva, Huahine
Sofitel Ia Ora, Moorea - Sofitel Marara & Sofitel Motu, Bora Bora.

Reservation in Polynesia : Tahitires - Tel : 00 (689) 41 04 04 - Fax : 00 (689) 41 05 05
e-mail : Reservation_Tahiti@accor-hotels.com

sofitel.com · accorhotels.com

general information

prices

Prices given in this guide are generally valid for one year. However, hotels reserve the right to change their rates at any time.

accuracy of information

Whilst every effort has been made to ensure that information provided is true and accurate (representatives of each hotel have furnished the photographs and facts concerning their establishments) no responsibility can be taken by 'Les Editions Sisyphe' for any errors or mistakes which may have occurred. Neither can the company be responsible for any changes made by hotels after the publication of this guide. Neither the author nor the hotels featured in this guide can be held responsible for subsequent alterations by the hotels concerned.

abbreviations

EP: European Plan (no meals included)
CP: Continental Plan (breakfast included)
MAP: Modified American Plan
(breakfast & dinner included)
FAP: Full American Plan (full board)

maps

The maps published in this guide are intended solely as a general indication of the location of hotels.

acknowledgements

Layout: Christophe Poujade
Contributor: Amelia Smith
Published by 'Les Editions Sisyphe'
Special thanks to Fred and especially to
Mr. François Bizot
Photos credits: Tonystone
p84 Mr. Dewey - p124 Mr. Matsumoto

No part of this book may be copied, reproduced or reused in any way without the prior written permission of 'Les Editions Sisyphe'.

further information

For further information, please contact:

Stéphane Fruitier
7, rue Saussier Leroy - 75017 Paris, France
Tel.: 33 1 40 54 71 19
Fax: 33 1 48 88 06 38
E-mail: stephfruitier@hotmail.com

Currency	Code	US$/1 Unit	Units/1 US$
Austrian Schilling	ATS	0.0653	15.31
Australian Dollar	AUD	0.582	1.71
Belgian Franc	BEF	0.022	44.90
Canadian Dollar	CAD	0.670	1.49
Swiss Franc	CHF	0.580	1.72
Cyprus Pound	CYP	1.572	0.63
German Mark	DEM	0.459	2.17
Spanish Peseta	ESP	0.005	185.22
Euro	EUR	0.898	1.11
French Franc	FRF	0.137	7.30
British Pound	GBP	1.532	0.65

Currency	Code	US$/1 Unit	Units/1 US$
Hong Kong Dollar	HKD	0.128	7.78
Irish Punt	IEP	1.141	0.87
Italian Lira	ITL	0.0004	2155.53
Japanese Yen	JPY	0.009	109.11
Mauritius Rupee	MUR	0.038	25.70
Malaysian Ringgit	MYR	0.263	3.80
New Zealand Dollar	NZD	0.484	2.06
Portuguese Escudo	PTE	0.004	223.18
Singapore Dollar	SGD	0.579	1.72
CFA Franc BEAC	XAF	0.001	730.95
South African Rand	ZAR	0.143	6.9650

The Most Exclusive Hotels in the World

Order Form

Please send me ...... copies of the 'The Most Exclusive Hotels in the World' guidebook at US$ 25 per copy.

* *Please charge my credit card :*

Visa ☐   American Express ☐   Diners ☐   Mastercard ☐

Card Number ☐☐☐☐☐☐☐☐☐☐☐☐☐☐☐☐☐

Expiry Date ☐☐☐☐

* *I enclose a cheque for the sum of* _____
payable to : Les éditions Sisyphe

Surname _____   First Name _____
Address _____
City _____   Postal Code _____
Country _____
Tel. No: _____   Fax No: _____

Profession _____
Company name _____

By offering one or more of 'The Most Exclusive Hotels in the World' guidebook to your best clients, you will be assured of exceptional advertising worldwide.